THE

CHRISTIAN DOCTRINE

OF

PRAYER.

AN ESSAY.

By JAMES FREEMAN CLARKE.

"Φυγὴ μόνου πρὸς τὸν Μόνον."

EIGHTH EDITION.

BOSTON:
AMERICAN UNITARIAN ASSOCIATION.
1874.

"Der Regierung der durch Menschliche Freiheit bewegten Welt ist nur möglich durch die Einwirkung göttlicher Freiheit. Diese Einwirkung giebt den philosophischen Begriff des Wunders, welches daher nur mit der Vorsehung selbst geleugnet werden konnen." — HASE, *Lehrbuch der Dogmatik*, § 150.

University Press, Cambridge:
Printed by Welch, Bigelow, and Company.

PREFACE.

THERE are two kinds of Prayer, the Prayer of Faith and the Prayer of Form. Men must either pray in earnest, because they expect their prayer to accomplish something, and ask God for what they want just as they would ask any one else, — expecting to get it; and this kind of prayer I call the Prayer of Faith. Or they must pray as a matter of propriety, and from a sense of duty, — because prayer is beautiful, or because prayer is commanded; and this kind of prayer I call the Prayer of Form.

Now when people get to praying as a form, — a proper, beautiful, excellent form though it be, — they will soon leave off praying at all. A certain insincerity is felt in such a work. We cannot go on with it. To speak to God, and ask him to give us this and that, — when we all the time believe that we shall get it not a whit the sooner for asking, but merely shall put ourselves into a better frame of mind, — is not sincere. It is not truthful, and honest men cannot do it, nor pretend to do it.

Little children pray the Prayer of Faith. They ask God to give them toys and playthings, and they bring their little wants and notions up in their prayers very artlessly and honestly. We smile, and sigh that we cannot pray so too. By and by they grow too wise to continue the childish prayer, and, like us, leave off prayer wholly.

Our ancestors prayed the Prayer of Faith. When the wind howled around their lowly huts, and the storm rushed darkly from the forests, — when the fierce Pequot and the savage Philip with his wild tribes of Indians lurked in every shaded dell of this fair New England, — when the crops failed and they were about to starve, — then they wrestled with God in prayer. They labored as men labor in ploughing a field, till in their agony of supplication they fainted. And when the help came, and the full-freighted ship sailed up the bay with its white sails spread wide like some broad-winged bird, then they believed most surely that God sent her in answer to their prayer, and no sceptic among them all asked concerning the time when she sailed from port.

But some time in the last century there arose wise men, — disciples not of Plato nor of St. Paul, but of Lord Bacon, — men who believed in science more than in inspiration, — and they could not pray any longer the Prayer of Faith. They studied the laws of nature, — they reasoned by induction from effect to cause, — they were experimental philosophers. Bishop Berkeley called them in his vexation *minute* philosophers. But they were good Christian men, and had not the least intention of denying what was in the Bible. The Bible said, *Pray*, and they said, *Pray*. Moreover, they had learnt to pray at their mother's knee, and felt the happiness of communing with God, and did not wish to leave off prayer. So they said, — "Pray. Not that prayer will give you anything you could not have had without it. But it will do *you* good. It will give you submission to God's will, patience, devout habits, and so forth. Pray, by all means, for spiritual things; for God will give you those readily in answer to prayer. But above all, *Pray without ceasing;* that is, be in a spirit of prayer always. Christ uses Oriental figures, figures of speech; he must not be taken too literally when he says, 'Believe that ye shall receive it, and ye shall have it.' God gives or withholds according to wise providential laws, and not according to our prayers."

After this doctrine had been laid down, and the Prayer of Propriety or Duty or Sentiment had taken the place of the Prayer of Faith, men, as we said, ceased to pray. They could not continue using solemn words to which they attached no real importance. "No," said they. "To work is to pray. Do your duty; that is the effectual prayer of the righteous man. Visit the fatherless and widow in their affliction. Keep yourself unspotted from the world. That is true Christianity; better than many Sabbath-days full of worship; better than knees stiffened by long hours of devotion. He that doeth righteousness is righteous, not he who for a pretence makes long prayers."

We live at present in an age *saturated* with these ideas. We live in an age turned wholly outward, — an age of science, of steam, of rails, and of telegraphs, — an age of cheap postage, and of all sorts of devices to make our outward life comfortable and joyous. Many run to and fro, and knowledge is increased. The Christianity of the world bears good fruit in attempts to mitigate the horrors of barbarous customs, which come down unmitigated and unrelieved through the ages of faith, — slavery, and war, and popular ignorance, pauperism, intemperance, and manifold evils. Strong, wise, and good men do not now go on their knees and wrestle all night with God in prayer; but they sit up all night by their study-table, and marshal hosts of facts into such shape as shall convince mankind what a mountain of ills they labor under, and how they shall throw them off. Good men of to-day — the saints of our day — do not dream dreams, see visions, commune with angels, they are caught up into no third, nor even second heaven; but they visit prisons and penitentiaries, they establish hospitals for the blind, deaf, lame, dumb, and insane, they labor to elevate public instruction, they struggle to make the laws more equitable. And for all these labors let us be thankful to God, for in them is surely to be found the Christian seed; they are Christ-like works.

But the effect of these doctrines as regards prayer, we see all around in other forms, not so good as those. It appears in our empty churches; in young men and women deserting the house of God, where whole generations used to bend together in awe and love, the old man with white hair kneeling humbly by the little child with silky curls, — where they used to pray *in earnest*, and go away refreshed at heart and stronger for any work, happier for any joy. We see it in sermons changed to popular lectures,— no longer earnest arguments, appeals from dying men to dying men, but rhetorical essays on some theme of philosophy, taste, politics, or social utility. We feel it, moreover, in the emptiness of our own hearts, in our secret consciousness that we are not acting out our highest nature, not living for the great end of our being, not growing into all that God desires and intends for us. We give ourselves to the world, though the world does not satisfy us. We labor to do good in some way to those about us, but we feel that, while we are ourselves empty of spiritual life, we can do them no real, no lasting good.

And look, too, at our philanthropic efforts. They are efforts, all of them, *in the right direction.* This age applies Christianity as Christ himself would have it applied, and as those ages of Faith and Prayer never applied it. I therefore am not looking for salvation in the past. I thank God for the immense advances we are making, and have made, in a true understanding of the Gospel. But with all this light, where is the heat? Where is the energy which once bore men from land to land, and heaped them by myriads around an empty grave in Palestine? I stood myself in a pulpit from which Bernard of Clairvaux in 1150 preached the second Crusade. "And is it possible," I thought, "that there was a power of faith which could carry Europe to perish on the hot sands of Asia for such an object as that, six several times, and that we cannot raise a Christian crusade to-day against our own great social evils? There, for example, is slavery, which turns our fellow-men into things, which threatens us with disunion, which tramples on the rights of men, which disgraces us before the civilized world. We, Philanthropists, when all our religion has run into philanthropy, and we say *to work is to pray*, — what do we? The most we do is to make a few antislavery speeches, hold a few antislavery fairs and picnics, circulate a few newspapers and tracts, and throw a small vote here and there for antislavery representatives. Luther, by himself, a man of faith and prayer, shook with his single arm the vast power of Rome, till its foundations trembled in every country, and its battlements came down in ruins through half of Europe. Loyola, another man of prayer, came forth, and by his single voice called out an army of tens of thousands to man those broken walls and rebuild those shattered bulwarks. Xavier, and Henry Martyn, and Swartz, and Marquette, men of prayer, circle the earth in their flaming zeal, and preach the Gospel to tens of thousands. How poor a thing is our Philanthropy beside their Religion! But let our philanthropy be animated by a religion like theirs, — let us not merely say, "*To work is to pray*," but "*Pray that we may work*," — and all their exploits, compared with what we may do, will be as nothing.

Every human being is an immortal soul in a mortal body. That mortal body in a few years will be laid aside, and will have gone to the earth whence it came. It is an organ, for a few years, through which the undying spiritual force within it shall be manifested and shall be developed. That spiritual force, that immortal soul, can draw its life only from God, its fount of being. Without a constant, steady communion with him, it is drawn down by its fleshly instrument, it is immersed in sense, it is buried already in the body which itself is to be buried in the grave. Inward, toward God, we must go continually for spiritual force, — outward, toward man and life, to exercise it. We *must* come to know and love God, the sum and substance of all spiritual life, or it is idle to talk of loving man or doing anything for him. We must have, to give. We must drain from an eternal fountain, from a well that never becomes dry, in order to water the smallest garden or plot of ground.

Now, in order to have a real energy of spiritual life, we must have actual intercourse with God himself. To think about him, to meditate upon his works and ways, is one thing; to commune with him, another. And to commune with him, we must have something to say to him; and that something must be something out of our actual life, something which *really* interests us, not something which we think ought to interest us. We must say to God something we wish to say, and not something we think we ought to say. Our prayer must not be made of supposed proprieties; it must be the "soul's sincere desire." Therefore, God, in order that men may come into real communion with him and so receive real vital energy, — faith, love, peace, joy, — has ordered it so that we may speak to him of our real wants, and of all of them, and by an earnest petition *do something* towards realizing those wants. Just as, when a man ploughs the ground and plants his seed, he coöperates with divine laws, the natural result of which is a harvest; so when a man prays for any thing he really wants, and while he prays endeavors to abide in the spirit of Christ and pray out of that, he coöperates with other divine laws, the natural result of which is the receiving what he asks. Not always, not always, in either case. The man may plough and sow, and no crop come; still, there is a tendency in ploughing and sowing to make the crop come. A man may pray for his sick child's recovery, and the child die nevertheless. But there *was a tendency in his prayer* to save his child's life. And in many cases, we may reasonably believe the power of prayer will accomplish what otherwise would not come to pass. We may believe that, if all those who are laboring for the downfall of social evils would work as much, and pray for their downfall too, — pray for wisdom, courage, faith, humility, with which to combat them, — they would speedily yield before this union of work and prayer.

One thing only is to be noticed. There are two conditions on which the full answer to prayer depends. One is Faith, — that is, to ask in earnest; and the other is to abide in Christ, — that is, to ask in a Christian spirit. The men who have lived in believing ages have not usually prayed in a Christian spirit, or with the Christian purpose. It was not the kingdom of God they prayed for, but their own success, the triumph of their own party, the extermination of heretics. Therefore their prayers, not being of those who abode in Christ, and his words not abiding in them, were ineffectual in obtaining their ends. The heretics were not conquered, the tomb of Christ did not remain in Christian hands. But because they asked in faith, they were themselves filled with energy which enabled them to grapple with all the powers of the world, or to stand amid flames, praising God.

But when the day comes that with *their* faith we shall also ask in the spirit of Christ, with his words abiding in our minds and hearts, then not only shall we have new powers of soul given to us, but we shall see God's kingdom come. We shall see war and slavery and cruelty, all selfish institutions and all wicked customs, crumbling away. We shall see Christ coming to reign over a world subdued by the power of Faith and Goodness.

In this treatise which follows, we have attempted to set forth some of the reasons of this belief; we have wished to promote and revive the spirit of prayer, by showing the truth concerning it; we have endeavored to show how Divine

Grace can be paired with Human Freedom, and Love be at one with Law. We have thus done something, we trust,

> "to overrule the hard divorce
> Which parts things Natural and Divine."

CONTENTS.

CHAPTER I.

PRELIMINARY.

CHAPTER II.

DOCTRINE OF JESUS AND THE APOSTLES CONCERNING PRAYER.

CHAPTER III.

OBJECTIONS TO PRAYER.

CHAPTER IV.

PREPARATIONS FOR PRAYER.

CHAPTER V.

METHODS.

CHAPTER VI.

MOTIVES AND RESULTS.

CHAPTER VII.

THE SPIRITUAL LIFE.

THE

CHRISTIAN DOCTRINE OF PRAYER.

CHAPTER I

PRELIMINARY.

§ 1. *General Survey of the Subject.—Importance of Prayer to the Life of the Soul.*

The religious needs of our time seem to require a new investigation of the Christian doctrine of Prayer. On this subject, as on so many others, an unreconciled dispute has long existed between the claims of Reason on the one side, and those of Faith on the other. The theological problem for the present century is to make permanent peace, and not a mere armistice, or suspension of hostilities, between these contending parties. This peace cannot be effected by the triumph of either party, but only by full justice being done to the claims of both. Not by ignoring or postponing the difficulties, but by fully stating them and fairly meeting them, can we now hope for any real progress, any permanent advance, in theology. Something has already been done, at least the foundation of the future temple has been laid, in the admission, now so universal among enlightened and religious men, that there can be no real conflict between Faith and Reason. It remains only to apply this principle, with unshrinking fidelity, to all separate questions of theology where the conflict still exists unreconciled; and among these, the doctrine concerning Prayer is one of the most important.

This doctrine lies very near the heart of Christianity. The two great principles which constitute the Christian life are those of accountability and dependence. Religion has sometimes been defined as the sense of obligation toward God; and again, it has been defined as the sense of dependence upon God. But if we consider the facts of religious experience, we shall see that the religious life can in no case come into existence but by the marriage of these two principles. It is only from the action and reaction of the two upon each other, that the life of religion in the soul proceeds. The sense of obligation, without the sense of dependence, produces only moral effort and struggle, — not life and progress. The sense of dependence, without the sense of obligation, produces only the fleeting and effeminate moods of pious emotion. But Christianity is neither a cold moral effort, on the one hand, nor a pious emotion on the other, but a life. It is a life in the soul, rooted in conviction, manifesting itself in action, bearing the fruits of love and joy. It is activity, conscious yet spontaneous. It is at once a happy growth and a determined effort; perpetual progress outward into the universe, to meet God more and more fully in the variety of his works; perpetual inward rest in the centre of the soul in full communion with the One Alone. Now this life is constantly fed at its roots by the sight of the Divine Law, which reawakens the sense of obligation, and by the sight of the Divine Love, which creates anew the sense of dependence. The law of God rouses the soul to effort; but no sooner is the soul thus led into active effort to do God's will, than it becomes aware of its weakness. And so it is led into the sense of dependence, that by opening itself to God it may receive from above the needed power. And again, the moment that it finds itself filled with new joy, new light, new power, it is moved to exert that power in the service of Him who gave it; and so the sense of power awakens the conviction of responsibility for the use of it. This is the natural history of Religion in the soul,—the Book of Genesis of the New Creation.

Hence we see, that, to any real Christian life, the sense of dependence is absolutely essential. But this in its largest sense is nothing other than the act of prayer. Prayer is essentially turning to God with the conviction of need, and in full reliance that this need can be supplied. Every thing else in prayer is outside of this, either as its consequence or its preparation; something secondary, or something ancillary. This is its heart. But to produce this full reliance which is essential to prayer, it is equally essential that we should see God as the living God, coming to meet the individual soul with special help according to its special needs. We must believe not only in God as a Divine Law of universal benevolence, as a great and bounteous Order of creation, but also as bound in a personal and specific relation with each individual soul. Without this conviction, the sense of dependence is passive, and not active. It is resignation, and not expectation. It is submission, and not hope. And it is only an active, expectant, and hopefu. reliance on God which so opens the soul to Him that His life flows into it steadily, and becomes its constant strength.

§ 2. *Present Tendency to undervalue Prayer.*

But there are, at the present time, many things which go to weaken, where they do not destroy, this faith in a living God. There have been ages of the world in which this was otherwise; ages which suffered from the opposite tendency; ages which believed rather in a particular than a universal Providence. Those were the days of miracles, visions, and preternatural visitations, — ages of Faith, but not ages of Love. They saw God inwardly, very near; as a special, and even a partial friend. They did not see him outwardly near, as the universal and impartial Benefactor and Father. Therefore, these ages of Faith have been also ages of cruelty, tyranny, and hard selfishness; in which man has trampled upon the rights of his brother. But the world has moved round to the opposite side of its orbit, and we are now breathing a different spiritual atmosphere. We have come to see God, with more or less distinctness, as the great Benefactor in the outward world: we see his benign providence operating for the good of the whole: but we have lost, more or less, our confidence in his living presence. Seeing him as Order, we see him in no other way. For such is the limitation of the human mind, that every new revelation of truth shuts out, for the time, some other truth; as the rising of the sun, while it reveals the earth, hides the stars. Thus the very manifestations of God in nature, in providence, in human history, and in the human soul, inevitably make it more difficult to retain the faith, so natural to former ages, in God as a living God, who hears and answers prayer, and who meets the soul more than half-way. The spirit of the age is in the air we breathe. It can only be shut out by the natural barriers of ignorance, or the artificial defence of that exclusive spirit which shuts its eyes to every thing not in its own creed. But such a will-worship, while it loses the advantages of its own time, cannot effectually regain those of the past. It is only the device of the ostrich, which hides its head in the ground in order not to see the danger. Despite such precautions, the danger is at hand; and it is better to look it in the face.

§ 3. *Spirit of this Age goes to produce the Sense of Obligation rather than of Dependence, and so weakens the Spirit of Prayer.*

What, then, are the ideas which, at the present time, tend in many to destroy, and in all to weaken, the conviction that God really hears and answers prayer, and thus, instead of the prayer of Faith, leaves us only the prayer of propriety, of duty, of sentiment, or of superstition. It is unquestionably the case, that, wherever the ideas and the culture of the present age have gone, that part of Christianity which consists in the spirit of dependence is not in equipoise with the other side, which consists in conscientious effort and the sense of duty. There is more of morality than of piety; more of conscience than of faith; more of duty than of devotion; more of obedience than of prayer. Men speak of duty and of responsibility easily and naturally, as of a part of their common life. If they speak of prayer, it is in tones of formality, as of something unnatural and far off, away from actual experience. Travellers to the East are struck and awed by the spirit of pure devotion often found subsisting with the superstitions of heathenism. In Burmah and Hindostan the people are seen with their faces to the ground, absorbed in the depths of prayer, inattentive to all that is passing around them. In all Mohammedan lands, when the hour of prayer sounds from the mosque or minaret, at morning, at noon, or at the evening twilight, all business is momently suspended. The trader leaves his bargain incomplete and spreads his carpet on the floor of his shop, the sailor on the Nile falls prostrate on the deck, and if you enter the mosque, so silent that you thought it empty, you find it filled with absorbed worshippers. Pass into Roman Catholic countries, and already there is less of devotion than in Mohammedan countries, but more than in Protestant; and in Protestant communities, the most enlightened, and perhaps we may add the most moral sects, are the least devout and prayerful. Why is it, that, as the scale of devotion rises, that of morality should sink, when we all believe that they belong together? Why is it that the most cultivated sects among the Protestants should be the most moral and the least devout, — that Protestants generally should have more of morality and less of piety than the Catholics, — that the Catholics should have more of morality and less of piety than the Mohammedans, and that perhaps the same law may apply to the relation between the monotheistic Mohammedans and the polytheists of the East? Various answers may be given, but one reason at least is this: that those views of God held in our age by the most cultivated tend to produce a greater development of the conscience and the sense of obligation than of the sense of dependence; and that those communities and nations, therefore, which partake most fully of the spirit of this time, partake also more fully both of its advantages and of its disadvantages.

§ 4. *Science, Phrenology, Ethics, and Spiritualism see God rather as Law than as Love, and so weaken the Spirit of Prayer.*

But let us examine more particularly those views prevailing among ourselves which tend either to prevent or to weaken the prayer of faith. All proceed from the same idea, fundamental in modern culture, which regards God's goodness in Order, rather than his love in Freedom. But while the essential view is ever the same, a view in which the prominence of Law conceals Love, it takes different forms, according to the pursuits and tendencies of individuals. Thus we have at least four classes of thinkers, all earnest and influential, the tendency of whose pursuits is to destroy all conviction in the reality of an answer to prayer. First, there are men of science, students of matter, penetrating in every direction amid the tangled phenomena of the material universe, searching always for facts and laws. These are always passing from general statements to statements still more general, always, by the necessity of their studies, removing further and further God's free creative act. We do not complain of this, still less do we approve of the charge of Atheism or of Pantheism brought against this mental tendency to substitute a more comprehensive law in place of the original creative act. If it could be shown that all the multitudinous varieties of minerals, vegetables, and animals in the world are but developments, by the operation of constant laws, out of an original nebula, this would not be atheism, nor any thing resembling it. For a law is nothing else than regularity of action; and when we say that every thing comes by law, we may merely say that every thing comes by God's regular and orderly activity. God is as necessary to carry on his laws, as to originate them; and there is as much wisdom, power, and goodness shown in developing a universe by a regular process, out of a nebulous mass, as in producing it by successive creative acts. We do not, therefore, complain that men of science steadily search after law, and behind the broadest law look for another still more general. We do not regret, but rejoice in, the tendency to see more and more of God as he manifests himself in the order of the universe. We merely say, "This ought ye to have done, and not to leave the other undone." We merely insist that this tendency becomes in practice an exclusive tendency; and that the attraction toward the idea of God as Law becomes an intellectual aversion from the idea of God as Freedom. Hence, among men of science everywhere, the tendency always is to a reluctance of belief in the supernatural and miraculous part of religion; that is, to God acting as Freedom, whether in creation, in providence, in historical Christianity, or in religious experience. Secondly, next to men of science who are students of law in the material universe, come those who study the natural laws of man, among whom the PHRENOLOGISTS hold at the present time an influential and important place. Phrenology, opposed alternately by ridicule and argument, has, in spite of both, made steady progress, and may almost be considered an established science. No candid man, even among those who disbelieve it, but may see reason to believe that it has done great good. It has called the attention of thousands to self-study and self-knowledge. It has shown them their weakness and their strength, — their peculiar temptations and their special capabilities. It has directed attention to the care of health, to mental discipline, to wise self-government, and especially to the immense results of education. Meantime, however, its tendency has been to teach human prudence rather than divine providence. All special providence it questions or denies; and a direct answer to prayer, to an earnest phrenologist, seems very often an absurdity. This is owing to the same cause as in the former case, the one-sidedness and exclusiveness belonging to the fixed contemplation of a single subject. There is nothing in Phrenology inconsistent with a full belief in Divine interposition, in a full belief of creation, miracles, providence, and the power of prayer. But as a matter of fact, in the present stage of this study, it operates like the study of science; and, recognizing the God of Law, it ignores the God of Freedom. Thirdly, the MORALISTS and RATIONALISTS are led to depreciate the free influence of God in answering prayer: the former, by the stress they lay on human freedom;

the latter, by the fact that every free act, whether of God or man, is, from the nature of the case, insusceptible of explanation. Human freedom is a matter of consciousness, and therefore is not often denied by the Rationalist on account of its essentially unintelligible nature. But Divine freedom, of which we are not conscious, which is a matter of deduction, and not of intuition, is often virtually relinquished by the Rationalist for this reason, as we shall see more fully hereafter. The Moralist, on the other hand, believing very fully in human freedom, fears lest its sphere should be too much limited if the Deity be regarded as exercising direct influence on the soul, or as giving except in accordance with well-ascertained laws. Fourthly, the SPIRITUALIST finds it also difficult to believe in a direct answer to prayer, because, while spiritualizing all of nature, and filling the world full of God, the tendency of his mind is to regard God as a Nature rather than as a Person. In all of these classes of thinkers, there is a tendency to deny any real, personal intercourse between the soul and God, and consequently to cease from the prayer of faith. Cultivating that side of the religious life which consists in active conformity with the Divine law, or passive acquiescence in it, they lose that side which consists in active dependence on the Divine grace, — that is, on God's free love.

§ 5. *Two Theories concerning Prayer which weaken its Spirit; — First, that we ought not to pray for Temporal Things; Second, that the only Answer to Prayer is its own Reaction.*

The cases in which these intellectual tendencies lead to a *denial* of a direct answer to Prayer are few compared with those in which they *disqualify* for believing in it. Our minds are so pervaded, so saturated, with the thoughts of our age and community, that they affect us unconsciously and involuntarily. Where they do not produce distinct convictions, they produce a *tendency* to believe or to disbelieve quite out of our power to control. Multitudes, therefore, who theoretically believe in Prayer, find it very hard to pray; the reason being, that their minds are filled with views and opinions practically inconsistent with all faith in any answer to Prayer. Thus, they find themselves in that uncomfortable state of mind in which their theoretical belief indicates one course of conduct, while their practical belief leads to another. Such a state of things is too uncomfortable to be borne long; for the mind of man is very logical, and always struggles for consistency. Finding it, therefore, hard to reconcile our conduct with our theories, we are apt, sooner or later, to modify our theories to suit our conduct. The result in the case before us has been the production of two theories concerning Prayer; the first of which declares that the object of Prayer should be only inward and spiritual blessings; and the other, that the only advantage of Prayer consists in its reaction on the soul to produce Christian states of mind. These theories we shall consider more fully hereafter. At present, we will merely remark, that the first tends to prevent Prayer by greatly limiting its sphere, and the second, by limiting its motive. Placed as we are, by the necessity of our earthly life, in the midst of earthly interests, a large part of our wishes, hopes, and efforts necessarily refer to these. If these wishes and hopes are not to be brought before God in Prayer, a large part of our life is at once excluded from its domain. In the best of men nine tenths of his waking hours are occupied with thoughts and hopes bearing on earthly objects. If these may be brought before God, then are they sanctified and purified in the act of Prayer. But if not, and he must only ask for spiritual things, then all this part of his true life is divorced from

God. Thus the sphere of Prayer is very much limited by the first theory. And if, according to the second, one can only pray for the sake of the reaction from his own prayer, and not in the expectation of positive help from God, we see at once how much of the motive to pray is subtracted. And as this method of self-improvement is a very awkward and unnatural one, and involves a certain insincerity, it must often happen that one shall renounce this method of magnetizing himself by Prayer, and adopt the more natural one of meditation and self-communion. We cannot wonder, therefore, if, where these theories prevail, the amount of Prayer should grow smaller and smaller continually, till it reaches its minimum. A sense of duty or propriety, or the instinctive sentiment of reverence, or the power of habit and association, may induce many to continue the custom of daily prayer; but its spring and motive force will be gone.

§ 6. *But the Sight of Divine Law may be united with that of Divine Love, as it was in Jesus Christ.*

If, then, the tendency of our age is to contemplate the Deity rather in the regularity of his laws han in the free movement of his love what remains for us to do? Shall we *resist* this tendency, and, to secure the advantages which come from prayer, renounce the light of our own time and culture, and turn backward to the ideas of the past? Not this; for this is to war against the providence of God, and to renounce those blessings which he intends the world to reap from the study of his thoughts, as they are unfolded in the vast order of the universe. Shall we then *submit* to this tendency without a struggle, and consider it necessary that, in order to meet God without, we must renounce his society within? Not so; for all human progress consists in carrying on with us in every new advance the whole acquisition of the past. Whenever we drop any thing by the way, we must, sooner or later, stop and return to recover it. It only remains, then, to gain that higher platform where Science and Faith may be united, and the knowledge of Divine Law harmonized with convictions of the Divine Love. It is not necessary that these should be separated. They have been from the first united in individuals; and the tendency of all Christian progress is a prophecy that they shall be hereafter united in communities, in churches, and, at last, in universal Christian experience. The grandeur of Christ's character consists in its being the highest harmony of all antagonist elements ever attained by man; that is, that in him dwelt the fulness of the Godhead bodily. In him this fulness was entire, making a perfect harmony, — a harmony which, from its very perfection, prevents our recognizing the distinct tones of which it is composed. Less perfect characters, whom we yet admire for the fulness and royal balance of their virtues, show their greatness by passing from one virtue into its opposite. One act of life shows courage; another, prudence. One utterance expresses their deep sense of the value of truth; another, the largeness of their human sympathy. From moods of noble pride they pass into states of tender humility. They give one hour to devout worship of God; the next, to earnest labor for the good of man. Thus we see in the alternations of their life faith matched with works, zeal with charity, piety with humanity, moods of contemplation with hours of action; and we feel that in this large experience they have developed their whole nature, and done justice to all sides of life. But the peculiarity of Jesus was, that he carried this fulness into every act. His zeal was wisdom; his truth, love; his self-respect, humility; his courage, caution; his piety, humanity; and therefore it is more difficult to distinguish these different traits than in a nature less truly harmonious. So we can distinguish the separate colors only in the sunbeam broken in the spectrum, and not in the white, undivided solar ray. Yet one may notice in Jesus that he always saw in God both Law and Love. His teaching, indeed, nowhere assumes the form of science; and it was no part of his purpose tc announce the laws of the physical universe. Bu in his whole teaching, if we regard it closely, we shall find him making a statement of the spiritual and moral laws of human nature, human life, and human destiny. It has been usual to regard many passages of this sort as promises, or threatenings. But they are, in fact, simple statements of the everlasting laws of God's moral universe, laws which are rooted in the very nature of God himself. Thus, in the Sermon on the Mount, what are the Beatitudes but statements of these Divine laws. When he says, "Blessed are the poor in spirit, for theirs is the kingdom of heaven," — "Blessed are the meek, for they shall inherit the earth," — "Blessed are the merciful, for they shall obtain mercy," — "Blessed are the pure in heart, for they shall see God," — he is not *promising blessings* with which he intends to reward his followers, but rather announcing facts which are eternally true. So again, when he says, "Seek ye first the kingdom of God and his righteousness, and all these things shall be added unto you," he states a law, the working of which we may see every day in the lives of those who, because they devote themselves altogether to the good of others, find multitudes in return ready to take care of them, and of their necessities. So when he says, "He that humbles himself shall be exalted," — "He that findeth his life shall lose it, and he that loseth his life for my sake shall find it," — "Whosoever hath, to him shall be given," — "Give, and it shall be given unto you," — "Nothing is secret that shall not be manifest," — "There is nothing covered that shall not be revealed," — "Many are called, but few chosen," — "He that is faithful in the least, is faithful in much," — "No man can serve two masters," — "He that believeth on me hath everlasting life," — and the like, — he is stating, not special, partial, or temporary facts, but everlasting laws, of universal application. These depend, not on the will of Christ, nor even on the *will* of God, but belong to God's most essential nature. Thus we see that Jesus recognized fully, and revealed plainly, God as Law; but, on the other hand, it was his special work to see and manifest God as a fre movement of Love. Never were the laws of God's holy nature revealed in the same *degree* as they were by Jesus; but his revelation of the Divine grace was one not only new in its degree, but peculiar in its *kind*. Jesus saw in God, not only perfect law, but perfect freedom, — Freedom, not acting against Law, not suspending or nullifying Law, but manifesting itself in a coördinate series of events and Divine acts, which, because they originate thus, are strictly miraculous or supernatural. Of these Divine acts of freedom, the coming of Jesus himself was the chief; for Jesus was not a result of human development, but the coming of a new life from above into the race. Humanity did not develop itself into Jesus, but the love of God came into the world to meet man's needs in the hour of his birth. All other miracles of the New Testament are secondary to this. They are the natural consequences of this supernatural event; and because Jesus himself fully recognized this fact, he stood always in that filial relation to the Deity which made him the Son of God. Because this conviction expressed itself continually in his life and words, he has brought others to God as a Father. He has thus made it possible for us to pray both in spirit and in truth; and it is thus that, when we have seen him, we have seen the Father.

§ 7. *To contribute toward this Reconciliation of faith in Order with faith in Love, is the Object of this Essay.*

Since, therefore, we find in Jesus a perfect union of faith in God as Law, and faith in God as Love, and since it is the destiny of his Church, sooner or later, to "come in the unity of the faith and of the knowledge of the Son of God unto a perfect man, unto the measure of the stature of the fulness of Christ," and in "all things to grow up into him which is the head," we must anticipate that "the hour is coming, and now is, when the true worshippers shall worship the Father in spirit and in truth." The time must come in which we shall worship God both as Law and as Love, in which we shall combine, with full conviction of the universal order of things, a sense of the personal nearness of the Father to hear and answer our prayers. Science and Faith shall then walk hand in hand, and the result of this will be a deeper strain of piety and a higher power of prayer than any yet known. For when all these antagonisms shall have been reconciled, no secret doubt will weaken the energy of supplication; no dread of superstition chill the fervor of filial love. Prayer, made calm by the conviction of its harmony with Law, will flow through the Christian's life as a majestic stream, without haste and without check. We see in Jesus what calmness and equanimity his piety derived from this full harmony of conviction; and so will it also be with his Church. The most fervent prayers of rapt saints and solitary anchorites will be weak and faltering when compared with the unceasing sacrifice of devotion which shall ascend from the Christian Church Universal when it shall celebrate the nuptials of Science and Faith.

It is the object of this treatise to do something to hasten this great consummation. By a new investigation of the subject, by a faithful examination of the facts, and a distinct statement of the question, by fairly seeing the objections and fully admitting the difficulties, we may at least hope to take the first step in the right direction. For the law of intellectual progress demands that the opposition of antagonist truths shall be fully developed, that contradictions must be fully stated, and every diversity and variety brought distinctly out, before there can be a final reconciliation. In this Essay, therefore, I propose to examine first the doctrine of Jesus and of his Apostles concerning Prayer. Next, to consider the examples of

Prayer in the New Testament. Afterwards, to investigate the difficulties, metaphysical and scientific, and the conflict between the needs of the intellect and the needs of the soul. Finally, we may consider the methods of Prayer, its helps and conditions, its results and advantages. The work is a great one, and needs, as Socrates said, a Delian diver. If it be the Divine will, we shall reach the bottom and bring up pearls ; but if not, and the time is not ripe, or the instrument not worthy of this success, even a present failure may be made the means of a better result hereafter.

CHAPTER II.

DOCTRINE OF JESUS AND THE APOSTLES CONCERNING PRAYER.

§ 8. "*Pray in Secret.*"

MATT. vi. 5, 6. "And when thou prayest, thou shalt not be as the hypocrites are; for they love to pray standing in the synagogues and in the corners of the streets, that they may be seen of men. Verily I say unto you, they have their reward.

"But thou, when thou prayest, enter into thy closet, and when thou hast shut thy door, pray to thy Father which is in secret; and thy Father which seeth in secret shall reward thee openly."

This passage is the first of importance in the New Testament in which Jesus gives instruction concerning Prayer. The substance of it is, "Pray in secret." But we must ask, first, What is meant by this command? and second, Why is it given? considering first the meaning, and secondly the reason, of the passage. Does it mean, then, as the language by itself would certainly imply, that we are *always* to pray in secret, always in the closet, and consequently that all public prayer and public worship is unchristian and wrong? That this is not meant by Jesus appears evidently from the fact that he himself prayed sometimes alone (Luke vi. 12, 13), sometimes in the presence of his three most intimate disciples (Matt. xxvi. 37, 39), sometimes in the presence of the Twelve (John xvii. 1-26), and sometimes, also, in the presence of the Jews (John xi. 41, 42; xii. 27, 28). Moreover, the Apostles, after his death, were in the habit of praying together in the Church (Acts ii. 42; i. 14; xii. 5, 12), and went to pray in the Temple at the hour of prayer (Acts iii. 9), and to the synagogues (Acts xvi. 16), no less than alone (Acts x. 9). Beside this, Jesus seems to promise a special blessing upon united prayer (Matt. xviii. 19, 20). These passages show that in this place, as in so many others, the literal meaning is not the true meaning, and that the letter must be modified according to the spirit, the context, other passages, and the great current of Christian doctrine. The passage, therefore, may mean, first, that it is wise and well often to pray alone as a test of our own sincerity and simplicity, in order to shut off outward, distracting influences, and to escape all thought of the opinions of others. Secret prayer is thus the best test of sincerity, of the reality of our faith, and the purity of our motive. He who can pray earnestly and happily alone may at least be sure of this, that his motive is not to be seen of men, that he does not pray because others expect it of him, or consider it his duty, or will think better of him because of it. But he who prays only in public, and never in private, has reason to think that his motives are wholly drawn from regard to the opinions of others. And, secondly, the precept may mean, that, when we pray in the presence of others, we should not pray in order to be seen of them, but should even then go into the secret closet and inmost sanctuary of the soul, and be alone with God.

The reason and importance of this command thus understood are obvious. So closely are we bound together, so much are we influenced by the opinions of those around us, so great a part of the motive force of life is derived from this source, that there is constant danger of its absorbing all other motives into itself. We can only escape this immense pressure by going apart sometimes and standing alone in the presence of God. If regard to human opinion taints even the solitudes of prayer, the salt has lost its savor; and the last fortress in the soul has been occupied by the Prince of this world. We see in the history of the Church how, notwithstanding Christ's command, public prayer has encroached upon secret prayer. Prayer in church has taken the place of prayer at home; prayer commanded by the priest, and reported to him again, has been substituted for the hidden intercourse with God. We see how prayer has been made a source of gratifying human vanity; how proud men have been of their gifts in prayer; how they have been praised for being powerful in prayer, eloquent in prayer, for making fervent and beautiful prayers, and the like. Again, we see prayer made a means of rebuking error, or of exhorting to piety; a weapon of attack, or a sermon. Men have prayed against heresies or errors, supposed to be held by those present; prayed for the conversion, or even for the damnation, of their opponents; and all this in order to influence the by-standers. These things show what a tendency there is to address the prayer to the congregation rather than to God, and how necessary still is this precept at the present day

The reasons for public and social prayer we shall consider in another place; but in closing our remarks on this passage, let us say that the proportion of prayer should be, that the *least* amount of it should be in public in mixed congregations, a *larger* amount in social Christian prayer among those who can all agree together and truly sympathize as to the object, and that the *largest* portion of a Christian's prayers should be alone. For public prayer must be expressed in general terms which are brief, and for those few general objects in which all can agree. Social Christian prayer can enter into a greater variety of particulars, and therefore be more full, since Christian brethren have at heart the same objects. But in secret prayer, every part of individual life and individual thought may be brought before God; for to him nothing is common or unclean: and thus, whether in thankfulness, contrition, supplication, or intercession; whether at stated hours or during all the moments of life, whether when alone or engaged in affairs; whether uttered or unexpressed; the sincere desire of the soul may continually ascend in secret to God.

§ 9. "*Use no vain Repetitions.*"

MATT. vi. 7, 8. "But when ye pray, use not

vain repetitions, as the heathen do; for they think that they shall be heard for their much speaking.

"Be not ye therefore like unto them; for your Father knoweth what things ye have need of, before ye ask him."

The vain repetitions referred to here as usual among the heathen, consisted partly in saying the same thing over and over again, and partly in unsuitable, minute, and protracted narrations addressed to God. Thus (1 Kings xviii. 26), the priests of Baal called on the name of Baal "even until noon, saying, O Baal, hear us." Thus (Acts xix. 34) the Ephesians cried out for two hours, "Great is Diana of the Ephesians." The Latin dramatist Terence makes one of his characters say, "O wife, cease at last deafening the Gods with your prayers. You seem to think them like yourself, able to understand nothing unless it is said a hundred times over." So, likewise, the Boodhists use a rosary with beads, by which to mark the number of times they have repeated their prayers. In the Zendavesta, or liturgic books of the ancient Persians, the petitions to Ormuzd, to the Amschaspands, to the sacred Hom, &c., are multiplied and repeated without end. In the use of the Roman Catholic rosary, the Paternoster is repeated fifteen times and the Ave Maria one hundred and fifty. If we ask, then, Does Jesus mean to teach that there shall be *no* repetition in prayer, we are immediately reminded that he himself repeated the same prayer three times in the garden of Gethsemane. Moreover, he himself commands repetition in two parables (Luke xi. 5–8, xviii. 1–7), and, as we shall see hereafter, *persevering prayer* is wholly in the spirit of Christ. This command, therefore, does not forbid us to make the same request again and again. It does not forbid repetition either of the thoughts or the words. But it forbids two things: first, vain or empty repetitions, in which the form alone remains, without the heart or the thought being in it; — and secondly, it forbids repetition as an *opus operatum;* that is, as something advantageous from the mere outward act, without respect to its inward life. Other things being equal, it also recommends, by implication, brevity in prayer (according to Ecclesiastes v. 2): "God is in heaven, and thou on earth; therefore let thy words be few; for a fool's voice is known by multitude of words." Martin Luther says, "Few words and much meaning is Christian; many words and little meaning is heathenish." And no doubt, in proportion as a prayer is sincere, spiritual, and earnest, it is brief, direct, and compact with meaning. In proportion as the thoughts are wandering, and the desire faint, words are multiplied, and the same thing repeated over and over in a new form.

We shall see the importance of this command by considering what a tendency there is to substitute words for thoughts in addressing God. One of the hardest things for man is mental concentration; one of the easiest, repetition of a familiar, customary act. It is Coleridge, we think, who somewhere speaks of prayer as the highest intellectual effort of which man is capable. This, it is true, is but one view of the subject; for prayer is essentially spontaneous and free, and so it is just as true to speak of it as the easiest, as to call it the most difficult of intellectual exercises. When we speak of it as difficult, we refer to the preparation for prayer rather than to prayer itself. The difficulty and the effort consist in that concentration of the mind which removes it from outward objects, from things seen and temporal, and fixes it inwardly on the living God, unseen and eternal. This being done, and the soul laid open before God, prayer flows forth a spontaneous stream. Thus it is a work of labor to cut a channel, or outlet, for the waters of a lake ; but when the channel has been prepared, the work is done, and the waters pour forth by a spontaneous motion.

But this preparation of mind, implying an act of concentration, of truthful introspection and of trust, is always a new effort of moral freedom ; a new movement, originating in the free-will of man. This is so much more difficult than any act of routine, that there is a constant tendency, growing out of the inertia of human nature, to substitute formal prayer, or the outward work, for inward prayer, which needs this creative act. Hence, quantity of prayer takes the place of quality ; regularity in the outward act, conformity to the established custom, external assiduity in ritual worship, is considered, on all hands, satisfactory. Not that any religion omits teaching that the mind should be engaged in prayer, but by the chief stress being laid on the outward act, the inward element of prayer is virtually passed by. Hence it is, that, where there is the greatest amount of outward prayer, there is often the least amount of Christian character. It is because the outward act is substituted for the inward spirit, and men are satisfied with the form of religion without its power.

The inward part of prayer, which is its essence, belongs, as we have seen, to the domain of Love and Freedom. The outward part of prayer, which is only a preparation for it, and not the thing itself, belongs to the domain of Effort and Duty. In proportion, therefore, as we inculcate prayer as a duty, instead of offering it as a privilege and Divine gift, we change the essential nature of prayer, destroy its life, and substitute something else in its place. We have already seen that the Christian life consists of two parts, by whose mutual alternation and reaction it is maintained, which we have called the sense of responsibility and the sense of dependence, and which are awakened, the one by the sight of Law, the other by the sight of Love. Now it is evident that, in proportion as we inculcate prayer as a duty, we transfer it from the domain of Love to that of Law, and thereby despoil it of its true life and value. Moreover, we change it, almost necessarily, into an *opus operatum;* for the character of all duty is that it shall be done at all events; done well if we can do it well, but at any rate be done. It is a duty to tell the truth: it is a duty to be honest in our business dealings. It is desirable to do these duties in a right spirit, but we must do them in a bad spirit rather than not at all. In the case of duty, therefore, the essential thing is the outward act, — the *opus operatum.* But exactly the opposite is the case with prayer; the essential part of which is the inward spirit of it. It is better not to pray at all than to pray in a wrong, unchristian, disbelieving, selfish spirit. We see, therefore, that if we treat prayer as duty rather than privilege, as effort rather than joy, as accountability rather than dependence, we are in danger of making of it that *opus operatum* which is forbidden by Christ in the text we have been considering.

§ 10. *Prayer of Faith.*

MATT. xxi. 22. "And all things whatsoever ye shall ask in prayer, believing, ye shall receive."

MARK xi. 23, 24. "And Jesus answering saith unto them, Have faith in God; for verily I say unto you, that whosoever shall say unto this mountain, Be thou removed, and be thou cast into the sea, and shall not doubt in his heart, but shall believe that those things which he saith shall come to pass, he shall have whatsoever he saith. Therefore I say unto you, what things soever ye desire when ye pray, believe that ye shall receive them and ye shall have them."

MARK ix. 23. "Jesus said unto him, If thou

canst believe, all things are possible to him that believeth."

MATT. vii. 7. "Ask, and it shall be given you; seek, and ye shall find; knock, and it shall be opened unto you: for every one that asketh receiveth; and he that seeketh findeth; and to him that knocketh it shall be opened." (Compare LUKE xi. 1 – 13.)

In these passages, Christ commands and encourages the PRAYER OF FAITH. The promise is wholly unlimited and unconditional. Whatever we ask in faith, we shall receive. But we have seen that other equally unlimited statements must necessarily find their conditions in other declarations of Jesus made elsewhere. Taking, therefore, the unconditional promise in Matt. vii. 7, 8 "Ask, and it shall be given you, for every one that asketh receiveth,"— we find that it is immediately limited in the eleventh verse, that we must ask for "*good things*"; or, as Luke xi. 13 explains it, for "the Holy Spirit," or spiritual goodness. But, again, the promise is limited by those other passages which require that it shall be the Prayer of Faith. It is not enough to ask, but we must ask in faith. Again, it is limited (John xiv. 13) by the condition that we shall ask "in the name of Christ"; which is also repeated (John xvi. 23, 24, 26). Again, there seems another condition implied (1 John iii. 22), that we shall ask in a spirit of obedience: "Whatsoever we ask, we receive of Him, because we keep his commandments, and do those things that are pleasing in his sight." So, also, James (iv. 3) says, "Ye ask and receive not, because ye ask amiss, that ye may consume it upon your lusts"; and (chap. v. 16) he declares that it is the prayer of "a righteous man" which is energetic and availing. So, also (Matt. vi. 15 and Mark xi. 25), it is declared that our prayer for forgiveness will not be heard except we also forgive our enemies. Moreover (Luke xviii. 1), he makes perseverance in prayer another condition of its being heard (compare verse 7), and in the same chapter, verse 14, *humility* is taught to be a condition of forgiveness: and, finally (John xv. 7), we read, "If ye abide in me, and my words abide in you, ye shall ask what ye will, and it shall be done unto you." By comparing together all these passages, we find that Jesus earnestly recommends prayer as the means of obtaining blessings which we should not otherwise receive; but teaches that, in order that the prayer shall be effectual, it must have three qualities. First, it must be true or sincere; that is, we must ask for what we really wish. Second, it must be in faith; that is, we must believe that God will be more likely to give because we ask than otherwise. Third, it must be in the spirit of Christ, which includes all the other conditions above enumerated. Now, we shall consider hereafter the meaning and necessity of these three conditions of effectual prayer. At present, we are only concerned with the second, which is the Prayer of Faith; and with that only so far as to learn what Jesus intended by it.

What, then, are we to understand by the Prayer of Faith? We have seen that it does not mean a belief that we shall receive, without conditions, every thing for which we ask. We can only believe that we shall receive what we ask when we ask in the spirit of Christ; that is, as we think, asking for every thing *not selfishly*, but so that in receiving it we may be able to advance the cause of Christ and prepare his coming. Even when asking for a private blessing, if we ask in the spirit of Christ, it will be that it may be used for public ends, that it may, in some manner, promote the real interests of the world and of humanity. Asking in this spirit, as disciples of Christ, whatever be the particular request, it will still resolve itself into this, "Thy kingdom come." It will be, necessarily, a prayer of submission also, including in it always, "Not my will, but thine, be done." Conscious of our own ignorance, and that we know not whether what we ask is best, and is really good for us and for others, this Christian prayer, like that of Jesus himself in Gethsemane, combines earnestness and submission, and of such a prayer it is not too much to say, that the promise of Jesus will always be fulfilled: "If ye abide in me, and my word abide in you, ye shall ask *what ye will*, and it shall be done to you."

But having thus stated the limited and negative side of the Prayer of Faith, we must go on to add that, if it is offered in submission, it is also offered in hope. He who prays, relying on Christ's promise, hopes to receive something because he prays, which he would not otherwise obtain. The *essential* thing for which he asks, he is *sure* to receive, and that as a consequence of his prayer. God always bestows something really good, something which will advance the reign of Christ, in answer to the Christian's prayer. Every earnest request offered to God, for whatever object, so the request be made in the spirit of Jesus, is a certain means of advancing somewhat the cause of Christ in the world and in the soul. Any thing less than this would not exhaust the strong language of Jesus.

He plainly teaches that every Christian prayer, without exception, brings down something from heaven, — that we always have something more because we ask, and in consequence of asking, than we should otherwise receive. Nothing less than this will satisfy his language, which teaches as plainly as language can, that not one prayer is breathed in vain; and this explanation is in harmony with every other expression on the subject in the New Testament, and is not contradicted by any other passage. We may therefore state that the Prayer of Faith is a prayer offered in the spirit of Christ, and in the full confidence that by its means something really good will be obtained which otherwise would not be received.

But the full meaning of the Prayer of Faith is not yet exhausted. Every Christian prayer consists of two parts, — one the temporal form, the other the lasting substance; one embodying our present desire, necessity, occasion, changing with time, circumstance, trial, or duty, and springing out of the occasion of the hour, — the other, the one constant longing of the soul for the coming of Christ, in truth and love, to overcome all falsehood and all evil. Let the Christian ask for daily bread, for his own health in sickness, for the health of another, for success in any enterprise; he asks for these that, these being given, some new power may be added to those influences which shall for ever exalt good above evil. Now we have asserted that his prayer always succeeds in obtaining this inward and most essential object; but we must add, that, if he is to ask for these temporal advantages at all, he must ask with the expectation that *they* too may be given in consequence of his prayer, that they are more likely to be given in consequence of his prayer than otherwise. For if not, then the asking for them would be a mere form, destitute of truth and reality; and the prayer ought, instead, to be confined altogether to the other object, and should never include any thing but the request, "Thy kingdom come." But in the New Testament we have constant examples of prayers offered for special objects with the earnestness which shows an expectation of obtaining the object by means of the prayer. So Jesus prayed for power to raise Lazarus from the dead, and obtained it. So he prayed in Gethsemane that the cup might pass, and on this occasion this part of the prayer was not granted, but only the substance, "Thy will be done." So he tells his disciples that certain kinds of demoniac possession go not out except by means of prayer and fasting. So, in reference to the blighted fig-tree, he promises that their prayers, when made in faith, shall be the means of their receiving what they ask. So he says that continued prayers may at last obtain what for a long time may seem to be refused. (Luke xviii. 1.) So, in the Book of Acts, we read that Peter was sent to Cornelius in consequence of the prayers of the latter, and that when Peter was in prison prayer was offered without ceasing of the Church for him. So Paul expresses the conviction of being delivered from prison in consequence of the prayers of his friends, and requested them to ask that special gifts of speech might be given to him for his work. And so James teaches that the sick shall be restored to health in consequence of Christian prayers. And finally, Jesus, in the same prayer which teaches us to say, "Thy kingdom come," teaches us to ask also for daily bread, — an expression which may well include all temporal wants and desires of our daily life.

Now, we repeat again, that to ask for these special, changing necessities would imply insincerity, unless we expected to receive them the sooner in consequence of our prayer. We therefore say that the Prayer of Faith must include this confidence also. It therefore implies an assurance that, in consequence of our prayer, we shall receive something really good which we otherwise should not, and that we shall be more likely to receive the very thing for which we ask than if the prayer was not offered. Whether this view be philosophical or not is a question to be considered hereafter, with other objections and difficulties. We now merely ask what, according to the teaching of Jesus and the New Testament, the Prayer of Faith must mean; and we, therefore, once more define it thus: a prayer offered in a Christian spirit for an eternal good out of a temporal need, and in the confidence that it will *always* be the means of obtaining the eternal good, and *often* the means of obtaining also the temporal need.

§ 11. *Persevering Prayer.*

LUKE xi. 5–8. "And he said unto them, Which of you shall have a friend, and shall go unto him at midnight and say unto him, Friend, lend me three loaves; for a friend of mine in his journey is come to me, and I have nothing to set before him. And he from within shall answer, and say, Trouble me not; the door is now shut, and my children are with me in bed. I cannot rise and give thee. I say unto you, though he will not rise and give him because he is his friend, yet because of his importunity he will rise and give him as many as he needeth. And I say unto you, Ask and it shall be given you," &c.

LUKE xviii. 1–8. "And he spake a parable unto them, to the end that men ought always to pray and not to faint, saying, There was in a city a judge which feared not God, neither regarded man. And there was a widow in that city, and she came unto him, saying, Avenge me of mine adversary. And he would not for awhile, but afterward he said within himself, Though I fear not God, nor regard man, yet because this widow troubleth me, I will avenge her; lest by her continual coming she weary me. And the Lord said, Hear what the unjust judge saith; and shall not God avenge his own elect, which cry day and night unto him, though he bear long with them? I tell you that he will avenge them speedily."

The object of these two parables is the same; to inculcate persevering prayer. We see in both of them an illustration of the fact, that only a part of some of the parables has a Christian meaning and moral; and that other parts are merely for the picturesque completeness of the story. The similitude in this case between the spiritual truth and the facts of the parable extends only to the two points of persevering entreaty on the part of the suppliants, and the final success resulting after a temporary, apparent failure. The motives of the indolent friend and of the unjust judge make, of course, no part of the moral. The truth inculcated is simply this: that an earnest prayer for *any* thing which we need may, for a time, seem ineffectual; but, if continued, may finally succeed in obtaining the desired object. The reason why the prayer is not answered at first, or why it is at last answered, is not stated. It cannot be on account of variableness in the Divine mind, nor merely because of the importunity of the suppliant, as in the parable. But it is easy to see that there may be reasons, which we cannot at present understand, on account of which that which cannot properly be given at first should afterwards be bestowed, without interfering with the Divine immutableness. Perhaps such a trial of our faith may be necessary for us. Or perhaps there may be some profound difficulty to be overcome, either in our own soul or in outward relations; some difficulty which can only be gradually removed: and so, though the prayer may have been effectual from the first, its effects may only gradually become perceptible. Let us suppose, for instance, that one prays for spiritual strength, for a clear light of duty, for composure of mind, patience, equanimity in the midst of trial, — this prayer may be answered from the first; God may immediately send some holy influence into the depths of the soul, which shall immediately begin to produce the desired change. But this region in the soul may be below that of clear consciousness; so that the change may not be perceived by him who is the subject of it. But if he continues to pray, more and more of strength may be imparted, until at last the benign influence rises into the consciousness and is perceived. If it be asked, why should not God do this whole work at once, rather than thus gradually, we reply, that the world of grace has its laws and its gradations no less than the world of nature, as Jesus continually indicates where he uses the regular operations of the natural world to illustrate those of the spiritual world. "First the blade, then the ear, afterward the full corn in the ear."

The limitation to this precept is found in the other which we have already considered (Matt. vi. 7, 8), which forbids the use of vain repetitions.

The perseverance which is recommended is not a repetition of the form, but constancy in the substance, of prayer. It is to maintain the same desire, thought, and purpose; to continue patiently looking to God; in a word, to *wait on Him.* It is

"Patience, to watch and wake and weep,
Though mercy long delay,—
Courage, our fainting soul to keep,
And trust thee, though thou slay."

§ 12. *Prayer in the Name of Christ.*

JOHN xiv. 13. "Whatsoever ye shall ask in my name, that will I do, that the Father may be glorified in the Son."

14. "If ye shall ask any thing in my name, I will do it."

xv. 16. "I have ordained you that ye should go and bring forth fruit, and that your fruit should remain, that whatsoever ye shall ask of the Father in my name, he may give it you."

xvi. 23. "In that day ye shall ask me nothing. Verily, verily, I say unto you, whatsoever ye shall ask the Father in my name, he will give it you."

24. "Hitherto have ye asked nothing in my name. Ask, and ye shall receive, that your joy may be full.

26. "At that day ye shall ask in my name and I say not unto you that I will pray the Father for you, for the Father himself loveth you, because ye have loved me, and have believed that I came out from God."

xv. 7. "If ye abide in me, and my words abide in you, ye shall ask what ye will, and it shall be done unto you."

In determining the meaning of these passages, which inculcate prayer in the name of Christ, all depends on the sense of the Greek word ὄνομα, and its corresponding Hebrew term. This expression among the Jews had a much greater extent of significance than with us. We are accustomed to regard the *name* of a person, or of a thing, as wholly arbitrary and a mere matter of convenience, having no reference to the character. It never occurs to us to suppose that there might be a natural correspondence between the name and the thing named. But among the Jews, as with other nations whose languages are less derived and complicated than ours, the notion had not yet been lost of a correspondence between the name itself and the character of the person or thing to which it belonged. Hence the importance ascribed to naming children.

Hence the changing of the names of persons, as in the case of Paul, Peter, the two sons of Zebedee, and others. Hence the significance of Adam's naming every thing in Paradise. It is only as we enter into this feeling of the Jews as regards names, that we can understand such passages as these : "Hallowed be thy name," — "In thy name we have cast out devils," — "To receive one in the name of a prophet," — "For my name's sake," — "He has given him a name above every name," — "Father, glorify thy name," — "Keep through thine own name those thou hast given me," — and a multitude of others. In some of these cases, it appears to mean authority ; in others, power ; in others, again, the spirit of a person, or his character. Perhaps we may say, that, when applied to a person, it signifies his essential character, his special personality, and his whole peculiar spirit. This character may express itself sometimes as power or authority, sometimes as spirit or life. In the case before us, therefore, to pray in the name of Christ is to pray in Christ's essential spirit. This includes, 1. reliance on his promises, 2. interest in his cause, 3. possession of his spirit or character. It is, therefore, strictly equivalent to the other expression, "to abide in him and have his words abide in us."

To pray in the name of Christ is, therefore, a very different thing from the mere formal mention of his name at the beginning or end of our prayer. It is not to begin our prayer with the phrase, "We come to Thee in the name of Jesus," or to end it with the formula, "through Jesus Christ our Lord"; nor is it to express in our prayer the intellectual opinion that we are pardoned or saved by the merits of Christ. It is not to express, as a matter of belief, that we rely on his atonement, his intercession, or his advocacy. All this we may do, and yet not pray in the name of Christ. For it is very possible that a prayer beginning and ending with these formulas, and containing quite a sincere expression of these opinions, may not include in its spirit, its aim, or its character the mind of Jesus. Its motive may be selfish, its object purely personal. And if so, it has no claim founded on this promise. It is not "the energetic prayer of the righteous man," which availeth much.

The one essential thing which is necessary to make a prayer a prayer "in the name of Jesus" is that all its petitions should have their termination in this one, "Thy kingdom come." This is the sense given to this prayer by the most profound interpreters. Thus Schleiermacher says (*Christliche Glaube*, § 147): "Whether one understands the expression 'to pray in the name of Jesus' to mean, to pray *in his mind and spirit*, rather than to pray from *an interest in his cause*, — or the reverse, — it is, nevertheless, impossible to separate these two meanings. For if we wish to do his work for man's redemption in any other spirit than his own, we must necessarily be intending *a different* work than his, and then it would be not *his* work which we bring before God in our prayer. Therefore, every prayer is a prayer 'in the name of Jesus,' in which, whatever it may be, one prays from the same position in relation to the kingdom of God which he himself occupied." So Tholuck (*Bergpredigt*), in commenting on Matt. vii. 8, says: "Both the subjective and objective conditions of prayer are fulfilled when it is offered 'in the name of the Lord'; for he prays in the name of Christ, who, on the one hand, *believes* and confides in him, and, on the other hand, prays in *relation to him*, so that he prays for that which will advance his kingdom." *

* So De Wette (*Exeget. Handbuch z. N. T.* ad John

Such a prayer, proceeding out of faith in Christ and his promises, and, wherever it may begin, always terminating in the desire that his kingdom may be advanced, is a truly unselfish and Christian prayer, and one which always obtains that which it seeks. When we look at all which Jesus says concerning the unconditional success of this prayer, when we notice in how many ways he urges, as an unquestionable fact, that, if we ask any thing in his name, it shall be done for us, we must be satisfied that he meant to say distinctly, that God always answers this prayer by giving that for which we ask. Such a prayer always tends to advance the cause of Christ, and to make his kingdom come. The two authors before quoted both admit this to be so. Thus Tholuck (ad Matt. vii. 8): "It follows that we may say, that all the prayers of him who prays aright are heard. As regards spiritual things, the result of every prayer, in proportion as it is believing prayer, is to awaken the spiritual life: as regards outward things, he who asks for them in faith asks for them in the name of his Mas-

xiv. 13): "'*Whatsoever ye shall ask*' is limited, partly by the connection, and partly by the '*in my name*' (i. e. *in my cause*, or in the sentiment based on faith in me and my confession), to labors for the kingdom of God."

er; and this implies that his chief prayer is, 'Thy kingdom come,' and that he asks for earthly gifts only so far as they are the means of securing spiritual gifts. Therefore, if God refuses the earthly object because it would be injurious to the welfare of his soul, this very refusal is a favorable answer to the essential part of his prayer." So Augustine (Ep. 34): "God is good, who, in refusing that which we wish, gives us that which we wish more," &c.; with which compare the fine passage in Augustine's "Confessions," where he relates that his pious mother, from fear of the temptations which might beset her son in the metropolis, prayed God to prevent him from going. Yet he went, and there became a Christian. And therefore the excellent Church Father says: "She sought of Thee, O my God, with so many tears, that Thou wouldst hinder me from sailing; but Thou, in thy deeper counsel, perceiving the hinge of her desire, didst refuse that transient prayer, in order to grant her lasting and permanent one." So likewise Schleiermacher, denving what he calls the magical view of the answer to prayer, nevertheless says: "Though we deny that what is given in answer to prayer implies a change in the original will of God which the prayer effects, yet just as little do we maintain that it would have been given without the prayer. For there is a connection between the prayer and its fulfilment, resting on the fact that both are based on one and the same thing; namely, the plan and method of the kingdom of God. For in this the two are one: the prayer being the Christian anticipation or presentiment developed out of the collective activity of the Divine spirit, and its fulfilment being the expression of the ruling activity of Christ in relation to the same subject. Thus looked at, the fulfilment would not have come if the prayer had not preceded it; for in that case, the point which it was to follow in the development of the kingdom of heaven would have been wanting. The prayer is not because of its fulfilment, as though the prayer stood isolated as an unconnected cause, but because the right prayer can have no other object than something in the order of the Divine will." *

This prayer in the name of Jesus is the prayer according to God's will (1 John v. 14, 15). It is the prayer made by those who abide in Jesus and who have his words abiding in them (John xv. 7). It is the prayer of those who are willing to forgive their enemies (Mark xi. 25). It is the

* *Christliche Glaube*, § 147.

prayer of humility, like that of the Publican who went down to his house justified rather than the Pharisee (Luke xviii. 10 – 14). It is, as we have seen, the prayer of Faith; and it is also the worship of God the Father in spirit and in truth (John iv. 23, 24). It includes in itself, therefore, all these separate conditions of acceptable prayer. It is the prayer of Faith, as it rests on faith in Christ and his promises. It is the prayer of Truth, as it asks for that which we really desire. And it is prayer in the Spirit, inasmuch as its object is not private or personal, but generous and large; being essentially, in all its various forms, a prayer for the redemption of man from all evil: and therefore, necessarily, it is an humble and a forgiving prayer.

§ 13. *Prayer without ceasing.*

The Apostles, in their Epistles, frequently refer to Prayer as a necessary part of the Christian life. *Unceasing* prayer is urged 1 Thess. v. 17. So Eph. vi. 18, "praying *always*," &c. Phil. iv. 6, "*In every thing*, by prayer and supplication, with thanksgiving, let your request be made known unto God." 1 Tim. v. 5, the widow is spoken of who *continues* in supplication and prayer night and day. Rom. xii. 12, "*continu-*

ing instant in prayer." Col. iv. 2, "*Continue* in prayer, and watch in the same with thanksgiving." 1 Peter iv. 7, "Be sober, and *watch* unto prayer." James v. 13, "Is any among you afflicted, let him pray: is he happy, let him sing psalms." Jude i. 20, "But ye, beloved, praying in the Holy Ghost, keep yourselves in the love of God." This spirit of constant prayer was a natural growth of Christianity; one peculiarity of which, above other religions, was to insist on a permanent union of the soul with God, and an immanent presence of the Holy Spirit in the heart, instead of transient inspirations. Hence Christianity is spoken of as a LIFE; as a constant, regular activity of the spiritual nature, — "the law of the spirit of life in Christ Jesus," — "eternal life abiding within us," — God and Christ "coming to make their abode in us." Such is the language of the New Testament.

Therefore, to pray without ceasing intends the unbroken union of the soul with God, so that all of life shall flow from God and to God. It does not mean a life like that of the monks or hermits, in which men retire from the world to devote themselves to formal acts of worship, and to make that the chief business of life: for such exclusive activity of the devotional element would not be as truly unceasing prayer as a life which alternates, like that of Jesus, between the mountain and the multitude. He who does nothing but pray is unable even to do this. His prayer necessarily degenerates into a form, into an outward routine, and so ceases to be prayer. When he takes himself out of life, where is the sphere of Christian duty, he loses the *subject-matter* for prayer. He has nothing to pray for, except in relation to the moods of his own mind, and therefore his prayer becomes wholly personal; and instead of praying out of an interest in Christ's kingdom, and the coming of his truth in the world, he prays only for himself. Therefore to pray without ceasing is to work for man in constant reliance on God; to work for Christ, and in every moment of need to look to God for strength wherewith to work. While this habit of intercourse with God is maintained, while we thus bring all parts of our life before Him in thankfulness, penitence, or supplication, we fulfil the command to pray without ceasing.

§ 14. *The Lord's Prayer.*

We find the Lord's Prayer in two places: Matt. vi. 9–13; Luke xi. 1–5. It is doubtful which of these two places contains the original form of the prayer. In favor of Matthew is the fact, that it is much abridged in Luke; and in favor of Luke, that the occasion for the prayer seems more suitable. We are not to suppose this prayer set up as a form to be verbally followed, but rather as a model in its substance, tone, and method. Attempts have been made to show that the petitions in this prayer were borrowed from Jewish liturgies: and even Wetstein says the whole prayer is made up of Hebrew formulas. But Tholuck has shown that this prayer was taken neither from the Talmud nor the Zenda-vesta; and De Wette, a very cold-blooded critic, remarks, that, "though Lightfoot, Schöttgen, Wetstein, Vitringa, and others have collected all possible parallels, even out of modern Jewish prayer-books, it yet appears, even supposing that the Jews have not imitated it, that the prayer of the Lord is by no means a *cento*, but contains merely correspondences to well-known Old Testament and Messianic ideas and expressions, and this too only in the first two petitions."

Short as this prayer is, it has usually been supposed to contain a great fulness of meaning. Tertullian says it truly contains the breviary of the whole Gospel: and De Wette remarks, that it expresses in its seven petitions the whole course of religious experience ; in the first three, the unhindered flight of the spirit to God ; in the next three, the hinderances opposed to this aspiration by the sense of dependence on earthly circumstances, and by the conflict with sin ; while the last petition expresses the solution which harmonizes this conflict. But it is well remarked by Tholuck that only in the mouth of the Christian does this prayer obtain its full meaning, since only the Christian can call God Father in the full sense of the word, only he can pray with right intelligence for the coming of God's kingdom, and only he can say, " Forgive us our debts, as we forgive our debtors."

" Our Father who art in Heaven." The word "*our*" expresses the sense of human brotherhood, the word "*Father*" the sense of childlike trust. Thus the two great commandments, love to God and love to man, are united in this first expression. The word Father is indeed applied to Jehovah a few times in the Old Testament, and the same name was given to Zeus by the Greeks, and to Jupiter by the Romans. But the sense in which the Heathen and the Jews call the Supreme Being "Father of gods and men," is different from the Christian meaning of the term in this, that they intended by it rather the original source and author of our lives than their present guardian and friend. The Christian use of the term implies the presence of a filial confidence (Gal. iv. 6). But with this confidence and trust, which enable us to bring to God our actual wishes, must be combined that sense of his holiness and infinite perfection which shall purify and elevate our prayer, and therefore we immediately say, "who art in Heaven." This expression, teaching us to realize the infinite elevation of God in his unchanging nature, of which the pure ether is the symbol, makes our prayer spiritual. When we say, "Our Father," we worship God in TRUTH, bringing to Him our *real* feelings; when we say, "who art in Heaven," we worship him in SPIRIT, bringing to Him our *best* feelings.

"Hallowed be thy name." Understanding by "name," as we before said, *character*, or the most intimate and essential being, this clause is an expression of reverence before the Divine nature. And this is the necessary beginning of all true prayer: first to recognize the holiness of the presence in which we stand, and then, in the contemplation of it, to seek that this holiness may be felt and understood more deeply by ourselves and others.

"Thy kingdom come." This, as we have seen, is the most central and essential part of the whole prayer, and constitutes the centre of *all* Christian prayer. The precise meaning of this phrase, as used in the New Testament, is open to dispute, and very different meanings have been given. By some it has been thought to mean a present reign of God in this world, and by others a future reign, either in this world or the next. Those who regard it as *present*, are again divided in opinion as to whether it is an outward or an inward kingdom, a kingdom in the soul (either of individuals or in the general spirit of society), or an outward kingdom in the form of a community, a church, a regenerated social order, and a reform of the moral evils of the world. And, in truth, the comprehensive term includes all these things, and intends God reigning through the power of Christ, first in the individual soul, next in a Christian community or Church, afterwards in a purified civilization and a world redeemed from evil. And this kingdom or reign of God, beginning in this life, goes on into the other, so that the two worlds are bound together and made one, and

> "The saints below and those above
> But one communion make"

Now he who becomes a disciple of Christ takes up, as his work in life, this work of his Master, and becomes one of that great brotherhood whose aim it is to cause Christ to reign till all enemies are subdued to obedience and gratitude by the power of his truth and his love. And as his aim, so his prayer. Whatever else he may ask, this deepest purpose of his life finds its expression in his prayer, and subordinates every thing else to itself.

"Thy will be done in earth as it is in heaven." This clause of the prayer has been sometimes interpreted as a supplication, and at other times as an act of submission, equivalent to that of Christ in the garden of Gethsemane. If the preceding clause directs our attention rather to the outward triumphs of the Gospel in a renewed society and a reformation of conduct, this refers more to the centre in the soul, where God reigns over a will at one with his.

"Give us this day our daily bread." By this petition we are brought into relation with the outward world of temporal needs; and this request, inserted by the Master in our daily prayer, is the one sufficient reply to all objections against making temporal wants the object of petition. It is bread, one of the humblest of those wants, — bread, one of the wants which we should, more than any other, expect to receive from work rather than from prayer; — "daily bread," to be asked for, therefore, continually; — "give us to-day," therefore, a specific and particular, not a general, petition. It is evident that this request will justify petitions for all the objects of temporal desire which can be asked for in a Christian spirit.

The word here translated "daily" (ἐπιούσιον) is one of those New Testament words which is not to be met with elsewhere in the New Testament, nor in any of the other twelve hundred works of Greek literature which remain to us,* and its meaning has been much disputed from the earliest times. Its signification depends on its derivation, which, in like manner, has been always a matter of controversy. According to one view, the meaning is *necessary* bread, or bread necessary for essential want; according to the other, bread for *the day*, or for the coming day. It has also been a question much discussed, whether spiritual bread and spiritual needs are included in this petition

---

* Tholuck, *Bergpredigt.*

with temporal, and the Roman Catholic interpreters translate "super-substantial bread," referring it to the Eucharist. But this last interpretation is extremely forced; while we may readily admit that spiritual needs are included in the petition with temporal. For if we understand the term here in dispute to mean that which is *necessary*, then, according to the symbolical language of Scripture, the whole petition would be for all that we need — whether of temporal or spiritual things — to make us strong for this day's occasions.

"And forgive us our debts, as we forgive our debtors." From seeking strength for outward work, we pass inward by means of this petition, and seek deliverance from the daily recurring sense of estrangement from God because of spiritual weakness. The prayer, so full of courage, which has asked nothing less than that we should do God's will as it is done by the angels, is also filled with the humility and the self-knowledge which recognize daily weakness and failure. How different is this from the prayer ascribed to Apollonius, who used to ask every day, "O ye gods! give me that which is my due." The condition attached to this request has caused a difficulty to interpreters in all times. And Chrysostom tells us that in the ancient Church many worshippers from fear were accustomed to omit this clause altogether. Others, like Zwingle, turn it into a profession of faith; or, like Luther, make it a vow to God; or, like Calvin, consider it as a warning to be merciful. But most interpreters more justly consider it to imply that, if our prayer for forgiveness is to be heard, it should be offered in a forgiving spirit. The meaning is, not that we must forgive others to the same degree with which we are forgiven, but in the same way and the same spirit. God forgives us a great debt, (Matt. xviii. 32,) "and we must also have compassion on our fellow-servants." The remarkable feature in this clause is that it should be found where it is, apparently breaking into the chain of thought, and taking the mind away from the contemplation of its relation to God, into that of its relation to its fellow-man. But this also accords with the spirit of Christian prayer, which is a spirit of communion, and with the beginning of the prayer which addresses God as "our Father." The whole of this clause implies the need of daily self-examination, to see whether we are at peace with God and with man.

"And lead us not into temptation." This petition involves two difficulties. Since temptation or trial is the necessary condition of human development, why should we ask *not* to be led into temptation? For James says (i. 2), "Count it *all joy* when ye fall into divers temptations, knowing that the trial of your faith worketh patience." And secondly, how can God be said to *lead us* into temptation, since not he, but Satan, is the tempter? And the Apostle also says (James i. 13, 14), "Let no man say, when he is tempted, I am tempted of God; for God cannot be tempted with evil, neither tempteth he any man; but every man is tempted when he is drawn away by his own lusts and enticed." The solution commonly given to the first difficulty is to explain the petition to mean, "Lead us not into temptation too great for us to resist." But the Christian, who is conscious of his weakness in himself, feels that any temptation may be too strong for him, and therefore prays to be spared, in a sense of his liability to fall. This self-distrust which trusts in God may make temptation unnecessary; for the object of temptation is, in part, to teach this very lesson of our weakness. Hence if we pray beforehand, in the right spirit, to be saved from temptation, then the prayer may do for us all that the temptation would do. But if, nevertheless, the temptation comes, we may be sure that we needed it, and may hope that we shall have strength to resist it adequate to the occasion. Thus the prayer of Jesus will be fulfilled in our behalf. We shall not be taken out of the world, but kept from the evil. That which would have been dangerous temptation, if we had not prayed, is changed into trial by our prayer; and by means of such trial, we enter more certainly into the kingdom of God. The solution usually given to the second difficulty is to paraphrase the passage as though it read, "Suffer us not to fall into temptation." But this is merely evading the difficulty, not solving it. The temptation is occasioned by circumstances which come in the providence of God; and if they thus come, does not he tempt us? The answer is, that, though the *occasion* of temptation is in the circumstances which God does arrange, the *cause* of temptation is in our own lusts or evil desires, according to the statement of the Apostle. It is apparent that the same circumstance which would be a temptation to one man would be no temptation to another. The outward act is not the cause, but the occasion, of temptation; and, moreover, when this occasion is sent by God, it is not sent be cause he wishes us to fall into evil, but because he wishes us either to learn our own weakness, or to practise and increase our strength. A wicked man may take a Satanic pleasure in making others wicked like himself, and may be really a tempter, but God does not thus tempt. He tries us, that we may grow purer or stronger through the trial. Thus explained, we see that Jesus intends, that, as we have recognized in the preceding petition for forgiveness our past weakness, so we should recognize in the present petition the possibility of future weakness, and in this recognition find strength: according as Paul says, "When I was weak, then I was strong."

"But deliver us from evil." As we have just prayed to be delivered from outward temptation, which is the occasion of sin, we now ask to be delivered by the Holy Spirit inwardly from the evil of a selfish heart, which is the cause of sin. And in this petition also is included the outward evil which results, directly or indirectly, from inward evil. This petition is opposed to a false optimism, which considers all evil as merely negative, and does not recognize the possibility of the soul, by abuse of its freedom, coming into a positive antagonism to God. If there were no real evil in the world, but only different degrees of good, this petition would be without meaning. Much of the philosophy of the present time explains away the whole positive side of evil, and establishes such a superficial optimism. But the deepest thought of this and of every other age sees more clearly that there is positive evil, as well as negative; that selfishness, hatred, cruelty, and licentiousness are not merely lower degrees of generosity, love, humanity, and purity, but their exact opposites, — that there is such a thing as dislike to goodness, hatred of truth, and aversion to God. This deeper thought is in harmony with the deeper Christian experience which finds in the soul a like antagonism, and recognizes the presence of these great polar forces in the depths of our moral life. Out of such a conviction, and by means of such an experience only, can this petition be uttered with entire truth.

The Epilogue. "For thine is the kingdom, and the power, and the glory, for ever and ever. Amen." Almost all critics, Tholuck included, decide against the genuineness of this Epilogue. The reason is wholly critical, for there is nothing in the passage itself inconsistent with the spirit of Jesus. On the contrary, it forms an appropriate close to the whole prayer, including in a few brief words its ground and aim. The *kingdom*, for the coming of which we pray, is God's; therefore, we believe that he will take charge of it, and not allow it to be kept back by the powers of evil. The *power* is his to cause it to succeed, for his omnipotence surrounds the laws of Nature and the will of man. And the *glory* is his, not ours; therefore we may rightfully ask wha' confidence in his power leads us to ask, with assured hope.

Such is the substance of this wonderful prayer; with which we may appropriately conclude our summary of the teaching of Jesus on this subject; since the prayer itself includes and illustrates all his teaching on this point. It is brief and comprehensive; containing no vain repetitions. It is filled with childlike trust in the Father, with brotherly sympathy for man. It is earnest and spiritual, submitting to God's will, and desiring that to be done, yet expressing the most common desires and needs of daily life. It is an humble but a hopeful prayer; recognizing the fact of evil, recognizing the fact of an entire salvation from all evil. It so feels the weakness of man, as to ask to be saved from temptation. It so feels the capability of man, that it asks to do God's will on earth, as it is done by the angels around the throne. It is a prayer which the lowliest sinner may utter, which the holiest saint cannot outgrow.

§ 15. *Prayers of Jesus.*

The instances recorded of the prayers of Jesus are not numerous, but are all interesting. After the great miracle of feeding the five thousand, he sent his disciples away in a boat, and went into a mountain apart by himself to pray. Before choosing the twelve disciples, he went out into a mountain, and continued all night in prayer to God; and when the day came, called all his disciples, and from among them selected the Twelve. Again, Jesus prayed on the Mount of Transfiguration, and came, by that prayer, into a higher state. He prayed before raising Lazarus from the dead; with his friends and for his friends, at the institution of the Supper; for his enemies upon the cross; for himself in the Garden of Gethsemane. These instances (which, no doubt, are the few recorded examples of a much more frequent practice) all hint at a connection between the prayer and its occasion. These prayers of Jesus all grow out of his life. After feeding the five thousand, the people wished to make him a king; and his disciples, he discovers by conversing with them, are convinced that he is the Messiah. He inculcates on them the conviction that he is going, not to outward triumph, but to suffering and death. He seeks thus to check the rise in their minds of false hopes. He then sends the disciples away across the lake, and himself goes into the mountain alone to pray. It is natural to think that the subject in his mind would be the subject of his prayer, and that he felt the importance of having these false popular tendencies restrained by new influences from above. When he prayed before choosing his disciples, it is probable that he had in his mind the important consequences which would result from this choice, and felt the need of being guided in it aright. The subject of his prayer on the Mount of Transfiguration we do not know, but its result was, that he passed visibly into a higher state, and a sphere in which he had communion with Elijah and Moses, and the subject of their conversation was his coming death at Jerusalem. The prayer at Gethsemane, so deeply interesting for other reasons, is important as regards our present subject, as showing that it was still possible, in the opinion of Jesus, that in consequence of his prayer he might be spared the approaching trial. Now this is the most complete reply to the objection to the answer to Prayer, taken from the immutability of the Divine purposes. Jesus had foreseen his death approaching, had spoken of it repeatedly as something necessary; and yet, at this very late hour, he did not consider it so immutably fixed but that it might possibly still not take place because of his prayer. It is impossible to believe less than this; and it therefore follows, that no event can be considered to be so absolutely decreed but that it may be altered by the freedom of the Almighty will.

§ 16. *Prayer of Jesus in John* xvii.

This last prayer of Jesus with his disciples, contained in the seventeenth chapter of John, is filled with a wonderful fulness and depth of thought and feeling. The cool De Wette remarks, that it is unquestionably the most elevated of any thing which evangelical tradition has preserved, containing the pure stamp of that lofty consciousness of union and peace with God which belongs to Jesus. The prevailing thought is his own union with God, which is to be a medium through which the life of God is to flow into the whole human race. He asks that he may now receive the glory foreordained for him before the world was, of transmitting the Divine glory of truth and love into the hearts and lives of men. He feels himself about to ascend to God, and that his power to conquer the sin of the world is now to begin. But as Jesus ascended from the world, and was outwardly to be separated from his disciples, he felt the more their need of being kept by Divine power in union with each other and with God, and this is the substance of his prayer.

The use and meaning of the term "glory" in this closing part of John's Gospel has perhaps not been sufficiently examined. That it means something very different from what is *commonly* called "glory," is sufficiently apparent. But what does it mean? If we turn to John xii. 20, we find an account of certain Greeks at the Feast who expressed a desire to see Jesus. The emotion which Jesus hereupon discovered arose, I think, from his seeing in this inquiry of the Greeks the two great elements coming together which were to form the basis of Christianity,—the Greek and the Jew. He saw the true religion about to be emancipated from its previous barriers and to overflow the world, and he was deeply convinced that this emancipation of religion which was to be his glory could only take place through his death, and therefore he says (verse 23), "The hour is come that the Son of Man should be glorified"; and adds, that "except a grain of wheat fall into the ground and die, it abideth alone; but if it die, it bringeth forth much fruit." He is evidently seized with profound agitation, and says, Now is my soul troubled, and what shall I say? Shall I say, Father, save me from this hour? But for this purpose I have come to this hour.—Father, GLORIFY thy name. The glory was to be this outflow of Divine life over the world, and Jesus directly adds, This is the crisis of the world, and now the Prince of this world shall be cast out, and if I be lifted up from the earth, I will draw all unto me. This would seem to make it clear that the *glory of Jesus* was, to be the medium, by his death, of uniting all mankind into one brotherhood under one Father. But this appears more strikingly from the forty-first verse, which, after a quotation from Isaiah, declares, "These things said Isaiah, when he saw *his glory*, and spake of him." If now we refer to Isaiah (vi. 10), we shall find that he had a vision of God sitting in the Temple, but his glory extending out of it, and filling the whole earth. As he looked, the door-posts of the Temple were moved, and the Temple itself became clouded and dark with smoke. Then he was told that the heart of the Jewish people was to be made hard, &c. This vision John applies to Jesus. The glory of God leaves the Temple and fills the whole earth. This is fulfilled in the Jews' rejection of Jesus, and the Gentiles' receiving him. Both had just been spoken of by John (in xii. 32), speaking of Christ being glorified also by the death which would draw all men unto him; fulfilling thus one part of the vision, and the other part being fulfilled by the unbelief of the Jews bringing the darkness upon them (verse 35) prefigured by the Temple being filled with smoke. The *glory*, therefore, spoken of, John xii. 41, is the glory given by God to Christ, and by him to his disciples (John xvii. 22). When Jesus glorified God, he also glorified himself, but not by seeking his own glory as his object (John vii. 18, viii. 50). Isaiah saw the glory of God and of Christ, that is, of God in Christ.

This prayer of Jesus is mainly intercessory. As the High-Priest entered into the Holy of Holies to intercede with God for the Jewish people, so Jesus, the great High-Priest over the house of God, entered into this "sanctuary of sorrow," this holiest of all, this most sacred hour of any mortal life, to intercede for his friends and followers in all time. He prayed that they might be one, that they might be kept by the power of God from all evil, that they might be sanctified by the truth, and, finally, that they might be with him, and see his glory, and be filled with the same Divine love which was in his own heart. Such a prayer could only be made for those who were willing to receive these blessings, whose hearts were turned the right way. And therefore Jesus says, "I pray for them, I pray not for the world, but for them which thou hast given me." A prayer for such spiritual blessings can be made only for those who are willing to receive them; for no Divine influence interferes with the freedom of the will. So Jesus prayed for Peter (Luke xxii. 32), but not for Judas. It is an interesting question what kind of intercessions may be made for the impenitent. (See 1 John v. 16.) Luther says: "It must be right to pray for the world, and right not to pray for the world. Stephen prayed for his persecutors, and Christ prayed for the world on the cross." That Jesus did not pray for the world at this time, but only for his disciples and friends, though on the cross he prayed for his enemies, was probably because he wished at this time to remain in the sphere of human and divine sympathy. In order that certain moods of mind may be entire, in order that we may advance far in certain spiritual directions, it is necessary that nothing uncongenial should break into the sphere of our thought. The aspirations of the soul to God, the communion of the heart with man, the investigation of truth, the assault on error, each demands its own congenial atmosphere; and when mixed together, mental dissipation and distraction is the result. Therefore, during this hour of communion, after Judas had gone out, the mind of Jesus was wholly occupied with the thought of his friends and their needs; and this period of sweet, loving intercourse was like the calm which sometimes comes in the midst of the wildest hurricane. For the time, all thoughts of a hostile world, of conspiring foes, and an impending doom, were shut out of his mind, and all was peace, all love.

§ 17. *The Prayer at Gethsemane.*

Jesus went out from this hour of holy communion with God, with his friends, and with the future, as one goes forth from a warmed and lighted assembly into darkness and storm. The thought of the coming fate now returned into his mind, and he went to the Mount of Olives, and to the Garden so familiar, to look that dark destiny in the face. Then set in upon his soul that great flood of mysterious sorrow which the Christian world has ever looked upon with such deep interest, and sought in so many ways to explain. It has been thought to imply weakness on the part of Jesus to shrink from a fate which he had so long foreseen; and it has been supposed to be inconsistent with his prophetic foresight that he should believe it possible for the cup to pass away. Some critics, therefore, have doubted the historical accuracy either of this event or of the conversation and triumphant prayer in John. But if we assume, according to the supposition just made, that Jesus had shut out, for the time, all thought of his approaching death in order to enjoy a full communion with his disciples, this subsequent reaction of mind will not appear unnatural. Some theologians of the weaker sort have attempted a superficial explanation of this anguish as arising out of bodily fatigue. Such explanations leave the chief difficulty unexplained Many theologians, therefore, have supposed that Jesus was at this time enduring mystical sufferings; that he was undergoing the punishment of the sins of the world, and was forsaken by God. To support this view, they have joined forces with the Deist, and argued, with Celsus and other infidels, that Jesus here shows less courage and firmness in view of death than many other martyrs of all times. To this it has been correctly answered, that a heroic apathy, like that of the Stoic or North American Indian, makes no part of the Christian ideal, and that the fortitude which is based on insensibility is not the highest courage. The divine strength of Christ was made perfect in his human weakness. He who sees and feels the whole terror of evil, and then firmly encounters it, has a loftier courage than the hero or martyr who goes to meet it with insensibility, or with a mind wholly occupied with excitement, and with his attention absorbed in a glorious future. Jesus was blinded by no such enthusiasm. He saw all the evils that were to come; not only his own sufferings, but those of his disciples and those of his nation,—the awful calamities which his life might have averted, and which his death would hasten. The words which he uttered to the women, on his way to the cross, permit us to look for a moment into his mind. "Daughters of Jerusalem! weep not for me, but weep for yourselves and for your children." He had no enthusiastic hope of a sudden triumph of the Gospel. He saw but too clearly, in the misunderstandings and ignorance of his disciples concerning his mission, how long it must be before it could be comprehended by the mass of mankind. Buoyed up by no delusive hopes, seeing the evil in its full extent and greatness, sharing with us all human sensibilities, Jesus recognized and accepted with truthful anguish the reality of the coming evil. But it would be a great mistake to suppose that the bodily pain of death was the chief bitterness in the cup which he prayed might pass away. The anguish was, that by this path alone his great end could be obtained, that all these elements of wickedness and sin should be necessarily developed by the course he was pursuing, that his work could only be accomplished by means of the treachery and cowardice of his friends, the cruel injustice of his enemies, and the murderous rage of the people. The bitterest ingredient of the cup was the SIN mingled in it,—the denial of Peter, the treason of Judas, the heartless policy of Caiaphas, the selfish injustice of Pilate, the brutality of the Roman soldiers, the ingratitude of the Jewish people. He saw all these black elements of evil approach him, and he might well say, "This is your hour, and the power of darkness." He might well turn once more to God, and ask, with the last energy of his soul, if there was no other way, if the same end might not be attained by some other means; if the world might not be spared this great crime; — and this was the substance of his prayer.

And yet there is a sense in which it may be said that Jesus bore at that time on his heart the sins of the world. For there is a law of the human mind which causes us to pass from the particular circumstance of evil into the universal cause. And this law acts in proportion to the greatness and comprehensiveness of the soul. It is but a small nature to which the chief grief of any evil consists in the actual amount of present sorrow. It is the spirit of injustice manifested therein, the discovery of a law of evil, the destruction of earlier confidence and hope, which is the sharpest pang. It is to find the law of disappointment, of failure, of bereavement, prevailing in life. Even the child's deepest grief at a trifling disappointment shows itself in the expression, "It is *always* so; I *never* can have any thing I want." And when we are older, and come in contact with the grief of others, it is not the particular evil, but the underlying law of evil, which pours gloom over life.

"She cries, These things confound me
They settle on my brain,
The very air around me
Is universal pain."

It is only by the operation of this law that I am able to explain the anguish of Jesus at the grave of Lazarus. It could not be merely the present sorrow which caused him not only to weep, but to groan within himself again and again: the present sorrow he would presently remove. But in that sorrow he felt and saw a symbol of all earthly suffering, of all human bereavements: he saw how death everywhere, bereavement everywhere, followed close upon life. And this large overlooking view of the sufferings of man he then took in anguish upon his soul. He saw then, with unsealed eye, what Paul afterwards said, that "the whole creation groaneth and travaileth in pain together until now." It is easy to shut one's eyes to the fact of evil, and look only at the bright side of things, and so we may bear it, — *but not conquer it.* Jesus saw and felt the whole amount of evil, and therefore was able to overcome it. And as at the tomb of Lazarus he bore the *sufferings* of the world, so in the Garden of Gethsemane he may have borne the *sin* of the world, — entering by one living experience into the very deepest depth of human iniquity. But this is a very different thing from bearing the punishment of sinners, and being deprived of the sight of God's love. The whole prayer at Gethsemane is to his FATHER, which proves that he was *not* deprived of the sight of his Father.

As regards the other difficulty in the prayer at Gethsemane, namely, its supposed inconsistency with his prophetic knowledge of his approaching death, we must consider the nature of prophecy in order to find its solution. The prophet does not foresee a future event as something absolutely certain, but *he sees an event approaching.* He sees the event in the future, and he sees it coming near. It comes nearer and nearer: it is just at hand. If nothing occurs to prevent it, it must take place; but even at the last moment, something may occur to prevent it, and it may not take place. The prophet sees the tendency of things; sees the direction of the approaching wave; sees it rising overhead, about to break in thunder and foam; and this he announces. This view of prophecy, at all events, is the only one which is consistent with the facts recorded in the Bible, and with such a prayer as this of Jesus. Continually in the Old Testament the prophets announce events as about to take place which never do take place. Thus Jonah declared that in forty days Nineveh would be destroyed. But the inhabitants of Nineveh repented, and Nineveh was spared. Isaiah went to Hezekiah and said, "Thus saith the Lord: Set thy house in order, for thou shalt die and not live." But Hezekiah prayed, and God heard his prayer and added to his days fifteen years. Nathan announced to David that he should die as a punishment for his sin. But David confessed his sin, and Nathan said, "The Lord also hath put away thy sin; thou shalt not die." We see, therefore, that the Scriptural idea of prophecy does not imply any iron fate, or any system of necessity, but leaves untouched the Divine and human freedom.

CHAPTER III.

OBJECTIONS TO PRAYER.

§ 18. *Metaphysical and Abstract. The Divine Attributes.*

According to the view we have taken, Jesus and his Apostles teach that both outward and inward blessings are obtained by means of Prayer, and that we may thereby obtain blessings of both kinds which we should not otherwise receive. But to this view of Prayer objections are made, and it is supposed to imply philosophical difficulties. These we now proceed to consider. We shall first look at the metaphysical and abstract difficulties based upon the Divine attributes,— then the scientific difficulties based on the laws of Nature,— next the psychological difficulties founded on human freedom,— and then the difficulties of the Spiritualist. First, therefore, of the metaphysical difficulties. These are found in the fact of the omniscience, omnipotence, and infinite benevolence of God. It is said, God is omniscient and knows what is best for us without our telling him, — he is infinitely good, and will give it to us whether we ask him or not, — he is an omnipotent sovereign, and must act according to his own will, without reference to our prayers. But it is evident that, if these arguments prove that Prayer is unavailing, they prove a great deal more, and prove that all effort in any way, for any object, is equally unavailing. Just as far as they have force as against the power of Prayer, they go to establish a system of Necessity, or, we should rather say, a Fatalism. If man must not pray in expectation of thereby obtaining what he wants, because God is good, neither must he plough, or sow, or build a house, or send a ship across the ocean. If it is best for him to have a house, or a crop of wheat, God is infinitely wise and good, and will give them to him. If this objection from the Divine attributes should be thus urged against such efforts, what would be the answer? Common sense would reply, God has established these means by which we are to obtain certain blessings; and if we use these means, he will give them to us, otherwise not. Precisely the same answer may be made to this objection, as urged against Prayer. It may be that it is well for us, according to the Divine view, that we should have a house, or a crop of wheat, provided we use the means, — not well, if we do not use them. So it may be well for us, in the view of God, to receive certain blessings if we pray, — not well, if we do not pray. The only question is, Has God made Prayer one way of obtaining certain blessings, as he has made foresight and labor to be another way? This metaphysical objection to Prayer is an objection lying against free-will altogether; and by whatever argument we defend the freedom of the will, by the same argument we may defend Prayer, so far as this objection is concerned.

§ 19. *Scientific Objections. — Laws of Nature. —Combe's Constitution of Man.*

The second of the philosophical difficulties which we are considering is founded on the laws of the natural world and the order of things. Men of science, accustomed to see law everywhere, and with whom all explanation is equivalent to the discovery of laws, find it difficult to believe in any real answer to Prayer, because it seems to them equivalent to a violation of law. They view it as a miracle, and they believe that miracles have ceased. According to them, God now does every thing in accordance with law, and nothing, in any strict sense, as a free Being. Or, in other words, they view the operation of the Divine laws in such a way as to exclude the Divine freedom. Moreover, as they see that the object of these laws is a benevolent one in all cases, they do not see how God could interfere to suspend their operation with any good result. For example, if a person should carelessly or wilfully violate the laws of health and become sick, they believe that his best interests would be promoted rather by his suffering the penalty, and so becoming wiser, than by its being removed in answer to his prayer.

These views have been urged, with much force and clearness, by Mr. Combe, in that well-known work, "The Constitution of Man"; * a work

* See Combe's Constitution of Man, Chap. VI. § 2, and Chap. IX. Mr. Combe admits that the moral improvement of man is one object of the arrangements of the world, but contends that the evils of life are always to be regarded as punishments for violation of the natural laws, and not as particular manifestations of the love of God to the individual. "On the whole, therefore," says he, "no adequate reason appears for regarding the consequences of physical accidents in any other light than as direct punishments for infringement of the natural laws, and indirectly as a means of accomplishing moral and religious improvement." The whole argument excludes all that we have called Special (or

which contains much that is true and good, and the chief defect of which is, that, while it asserts prudence, it rejects Providence. It gives us a true, but one-sided, view of the world and of life. Like most partial systems, it is inexhaustible in explanation. From its point of view every thing is explained; all the evils of life find a solution. Only, after the understanding has been gratified by the crystal clearness of this stream of thought, there is some deeper instinct which grows dissatisfied with its shallowness. Nothing is more easy than to explain all the most difficult problems of the universe, provided you omit to notice the facts on one side of the question. This book of Mr. Combe has had immense popularity with a certain class of minds, on account of its fertility in explanations, and its practical wisdom. To great multitudes, in fact, it has taken the place of the New Testament, as the guide of life. A useful book, no doubt, on the whole, but one the defects of which should be pointed out. These defects, as far as we are now concerned with them, consist in the denial of Providence. We do not mean

---

particular) Providence. As regards Prayer, Mr. Combe contends that its efficacy is only on the mind of the supplicant, according to the view to be considered by us further on.

that Mr. Combe denies what is usually called General Providence, for this he teaches in the strongest manner. That is, he teaches that, while the universe is controlled everywhere by laws, these laws have always a benevolent object. They are intended to do good, and they work good to races and classes always, though individuals are sometimes sacrificed for the good of the whole. Thus, for example, it is a law of God that fire should burn and inflict great pain on the human body if exposed to it, and this is for the advantage of men, inasmuch as the pain is a warning to them to avoid this injury. But sometimes it happens that an individual may, without any fault, be seriously injured, and in this case, according to Mr. Combe, he is sacrificed for the good of the whole. It is something which cannot be helped, for such exceptions are inevitable in the working of all general laws. This is the doctrine of a General Providence. It is true as far as it goes, but it does not satisfy the needs of the religious mind. It does not accord with the doctrine of Jesus concerning the fatherly character of God, and his attention to details, his care for the lowliest individuals, no less than for the progress of the whole. According to the teaching of Jesus, we are led to believe that all the events which befall us have a special meaning, and a special value for ourselves. If we stop where Mr. Combe stops, while the Divine benevolence toward the race is maintained, the fatherly love of God for the individual is wholly omitted. Now we do not wish to deny the General Providence asserted by Mr. Combe. We accept his whole theory on its positive side, but omit its negations. For we have learned that the errors of almost every theory or system consist rather in what it rejects than in what it asserts, rather in its negations than its positions. In other words, the chief source of human error is not in the perversity, but rather in the limitations of the human intellect. One mind standing in a certain position sees one part of truth, and hastily rejects that part which from his present position he is unable to perceive. Others, standing in a different place, see another side of truth, and perhaps, in asserting it, reject as hastily as the first that seen by others. Thus, if we could add together the assertions of different systems, and cancel their negations, we should come nearer to a perfect view of truth than in any other way. Thus, in the case before us, Mr. Combe and a certain class of minds, see God working by general laws, for the good of the whole. Another class of minds are led by their religious instincts, and by the language of the New Testament, to see God as the Friend of the individual, sending special blessings to meet special occasions. Is there any reason why these views should not be united? Are they necessarily inconsistent with each other? May not every event which takes place flow both from general providence, and also from particular providence, being in accordance with laws made for the good of the whole, and yet having a special meaning and value for the individual. Even a wise, kind parent, while enforcing laws in the family necessary for the comfort of the household, is able also to make them operate for the advantage of the individual child. How much more may the Infinitely Wise One be able to do this! And if He is able to do it, certainly He must wish to do it. If the individual is ever sacrificed, in the slightest degree, for the good of the whole, it must be because the Deity cannot help it. But the possibility of such a union of good to the whole and good to the individual was believed by the wise, even before Jesus taught that "not a sparrow falls without our Father," and that "every hair" of our head "is numbered." While we find in modern times one class contending that all events happen by *natural* laws, and that therefore there is nothing *supernatural* about them, and another class contending that *some* events have a supernatural source, and therefore are not according to natural laws, the wiser ancients were willing to admit that events could be at once natural and supernatural. Thus Plutarch says * (speaking of those who were ancients and moderns to him): "The men of old directed their attention simply to the divine in phenomena; as God is the beginning and centre of all, and from him all things proceed; and they overlooked natural causes. The moderns turned themselves wholly away from that divine ground of things, and supposed every thing could be explained from natural causes. Both these views are, however, partial and defective, and the right understanding of the matter requires that both should be combined." So too Hippocrates,† a contemporary of Socrates, denied the discrepancy between the natural and the supernatural, and treated all phenomena as at once divine and also scientifically determinable. "All diseases," he says, "are divine, yet each has its own physical condition. All are from God, but none are with-

* Quoted in Neander's Church History (Torrey's translation), Vol. I. p. 23.

† Quoted by Grote, History of Greece, Vol. I. p. 370 (Boston edition).

out Nature." Thus, wiser than some of us, these deep thinkers knew

> "How to o'errule the hard divorce,
> Which parts things natural and divine."

The difficulty thus urged as an objection to all special providence applies with equal force to any real answer to Prayer, and those who find difficulty in the former doctrine will find an equal difficulty in the latter. But we maintain that we may believe in God acting through natural laws for the general good of races, and also in God acting supernaturally in the sphere of Freedom for the special needs of individuals. When it is objected, that all such supernatural action implies a miracle, and that the days of miracles have ceased, we must ask in turn for the true meaning of a miracle. If a miracle means a violation or suspension of the laws of nature, then there would be a real contradiction between the Supernatural and the Natural, and belief in the one would so far nullify belief in the other. But if, as the better theologians of all schools maintain, a miracle is no violation of a law of nature, but the coming in of a new force from a higher sphere, which, while the old force, or law, works on, controls it according to the special need, then there is no such contradiction. We may believe at the same time in God's natural and supernatural action. We may believe in general and special providence. We may believe in the natural laws and also in the answer to Prayer. For, according to this view, miracles have not ceased, and never will cease until the God of Christianity abandons the world, and until living faith is no more found on the earth. For all Christian life is supernatural, flowing from a higher fountain than any on earth. It is a life hid with Christ in God. Therefore Luther contended that the true miracle of Christianity was the creation of spiritual life in the human soul, compared with which such outward miracles as the healing of the sick and walking on the water were quite secondary and unimportant.

If we suppose, accordingly, that God steadily maintains the order of the universe and the laws of nature, but that beside this he continually sends new and special influences into the world of matter and of mind to meet the rising exigencies of the hour, and that this is no afterthought, but part of the great plan of the universe from the beginning, the conflict between the Natural and Supernatural falls to the ground. That God does influence the world from a realm of freedom by ever-new creative activity, no less than from a realm of law, is not only asserted by Christian faith and needed by the human heart, but is demanded by the deepest philosophy. Thus Hase, a most clear-headed thinker, of the latest school of German thought, declares: "The government of a world, actuated by human freedom, is only possible by means of an inworking of Divine freedom. This inworking gives us the philosophical notion of a miracle, which therefore can only be denied with the denial of Providence itself."* And if we believe in human freedom, we have before our eyes the constant proof that the Natural can coexist and coöperate with the Supernatural. For human freedom is in the strictest sense a force which acts within nature, but from above nature. It is surrounded by laws, and limited externally by the laws of organization and circumstances, but it cannot itself be brought under law. Every act of freedom is a new creation, and wholly inexplicable. The moment that you explain it as resulting from any thing already in existence, you deny Freedom, and introduce Necessity. The moment you make outward motives to be the cause of our

* Hase, *Lehrbuch der Dogmatik*, § 150.

actions, and not merely the occasions, you deny, so far, human freedom. If this view be true, then every human being is himself an illustration of the coexistence and harmony of the Natural and the Supernatural. Part of his life is natural, resulting from organic tendencies, determined by external motives, and another part is supernatural, the reaction of the free will and the power of choice. If man, therefore, himself can act in this world at the same time in a sphere of Freedom and of Law, shall we deny a like capacity to God, and limit his activity to the support of existing laws? Much rather must the adequate view of the Deity suppose in Him the perfect harmony and absolute synthesis of law and freedom, — an infinite, creative activity, for ever combined with an unchanging support of the never-failing laws of the universe.

But if, after all, we cannot fathom the depth of this mystery, we may console ourselves by such thoughts as these, which we commend to our friends for their refreshment: —

"No human eyes Thy face may see;
No human thought Thy form may know;
But all creation dwells in Thee,
And Thy great Life through all doth flow!

And yet, O strange and wondrous thought!
Thou art a God who hearest prayer,
And every heart with sorrow fraught
To seek thy present aid may dare.

"And though most weak our efforts seem
Into one creed these thoughts to bind,
And vain the intellectual dream
To see and know the Eternal Mind,—

"Yet Thou wilt turn them not aside
Who cannot solve Thy life divine,
But would give up all reason's pride
To know their hearts approved by Thine." *

The objection, that it is better for us always to suffer the penalty resulting from an infraction of natural laws, than to have this penalty removed in answer to Prayer, requires a moment's consideration. True, the object of the penalty is benevolent, and its tendency on the whole is beneficial. But when your child has burned himself, do you refuse to apply alleviation on this account? Do you think it better that he should suffer the penalty to the full amount, or do you not rather hasten to the physician for relief? And if you

* These beautiful lines first appeared in the "Book of Hymns," published by Ticknor & Co., Boston, and were written, we think, by Rev. T. W. Higginson.

know or believe that relief can also be obtained through Prayer, why not apply for it?

§ 20. *Psychological Objections. Human Freedom.*

The next supposed objection to the efficacy of Prayer which we have to consider, is that derived from the fact of human freedom. This objection is brought against any influence exerted by God directly on the human soul in answer to Prayer. It is argued, that such influence would interfere with human liberty. But to this objection there are two replies. First, that an influence exerted on the soul by God because we have asked for it, is of course an influence which we ourselves freely choose to receive. It is not given against our will, or without our consent. How, then, can it interfere with our freedom? And secondly, this influence is not to be considered, in any case, as compulsory. No Divine influence is irresistible; no such influence paralyzes the soul, or moves it, as a material substance is moved by an outward force. We are not controlled by the Holy Spirit as the Jesuit was by his rule to be controlled by his superior, — blindly, passively, like a corpse. All Divine influence rouses, rather than represses, the activity of the soul, develops its individuality, quickens its freedom. And do we not see that the law of influence is universal? Every man whom we meet influences us, and we him. No one speaks to us, or even looks at us, but there is an influence for good or evil exerted by his character upon ours. His character, or his transient mood, acts immediately upon ours. It expresses itself, not only in his words and actions, but in the tone of his voice and the expression of his eye. A serious, earnest man, a generous, kindly man, a truthful and sincere man, expresses these qualities by his whole manner and demeanor. Light flows from him, sunny light, to illuminate and cheer his whole horizon. In like manner, a worldly man, a sensualist, a selfish, hard-hearted man, one who habitually sneers at every thing noble and pure, rays out darkness like the wandering stars of the Apostle. Thus influence goes from us, falls from us with every word we speak, with every breath we draw. The orator is addressing an audience of a thousand persons, and he sees some one coming in whose opinions and feelings he is acquainted with, and the presence of that single person modifies a little what he is about to say, or his manner of saying it. Thus are we surrounded from childhood to the grave by influences, for good or evil perpetually acting upon us, not irresistible indeed, but inevitable; and since every thing else thus influences us, shall God be the only being whose influence must be excluded? Shall He exert no influence upon the souls of his children, to turn them from evil or lead them to good? Shall we fear that his influence, exerted in answer to Prayer, will interfere with our freedom, when our freedom remains to us in spite of all this ocean of influence flowing over us from every quarter and at every moment?

§ 21. *Transcendental Objections.*

There is also a spiritual philosophy, which, by its view of God and of man, tends to a distrust in the efficacy of Prayer. Its view of God tends to Pantheism, its view of Man to Stoicism. It rejects from its idea of God the element of personality, and regards him rather as essential Being and the most abstract Spirit than as a personal Father. It fears to degrade God by making him too much like ourselves, and shrinks from direct communion with him, as implying anthropomorphism. It dreads lest the pure and spiritual idea of God should be degraded by being mixed up with low desires and earthly cares. Its worship is adoration and submission, rather than supplication; and its view of man is also opposed to any expectation of an answer to Prayer. Man, according to this philosophy, stands in the midst of the mighty and relentless forces of Nature, to make himself strong by patience, resolution, and unflinching fortitude. The wheels of Nature thunder on along their fixed path from century to century, and he who falls on them is broken while him whom they strike down is ground to powder. It is of no use to ask for mercy, for Nature gives no quarter. Her face, full of stony beauty, looks out relentless, with features unchanging as those of the Egyptian Sphinx. Man can only triumph over Fate by knowing it and bearing it. When he has made up his mind to acquiesce in events as they come, in things as they are, he has secured the highest moral triumph. It is easy to see how inevitably such a view of God, and such a theory of man and of human life, must tend to check all earnest prayer.

In opposition to this view of life, so beautiful but so cold, we present the attitude assumed by Jesus toward God and toward life. He who said to the woman of Samaria, "God is Spirit," also taught his disciples to say, "Our Father." He who made it the centre of all supplication to pray that God's will should be done on earth as in heaven, taught us in the next petition to ask for our daily bread. He who demanded, in view of the great emergencies and risks of life, a readiness for entire self-renunciation as the first condition of discipleship, nevertheless encouraged his followers to bring every desire of their heart before God. As the entrance fee into his school, he demanded that they should be ready to hate father and mother, to give all their wealth away, to leave every thing, and to take up their cross. But having been found equal to this test, he laid on them no ascetic discipline, took them not away from the common scenes of life, and lived with them in cheerful communion with God and man. God was to him always the nearest friend; and life was no fatal web, but a scene where, amid the steady operation of divine laws, there was still the freest scope for divine and human freedom. We conceive that it is only necessary to compare these two views of God and Nature, to see how much more large and human that of Christ is than the spiritual Stoicism we have been considering.

§ 22. *Prayer a Reaction. — Objections to this Theory.*

To evade these supposed difficulties, two theories have been very generally adopted in reference to Prayer, which we will proceed to consider. The first denies all real influence from Prayer, except upon the soul itself in the way of reaction. It is supposed that the only benefit of Prayer is the effect which it exerts upon the mind of the supplicant by its natural reaction. When he prays, his prayer affects himself, and not God. He asks for humility, and in the very act of asking makes himself humble. He asks for submission, and so puts himself into a submissive state of mind. According to this view, if we ask for any outward mercy, it must be in the most general terms, and then merely to create in our own minds confidence in the providential care of God. If we intercede for others, it is merely to create in our own hearts feelings of sympathy and good-will towards them. Thus, a Doctor of Divinity and Professor of Theology in the College of Glasgow writes, in the middle of the last century: "God is not wrought upon and changed by our prayers. Prayer only works its effect upon us as it contributes to change the temper of our minds, to beget or improve right dispositions in them," &c. The writer, being accused of heresy for these views, was condemned by the Presbytery. He appealed to the Synod, and was acquitted, and the General Assembly refused to alter the judgment of the Synod. The same view is taught by Dr. Blair, who says: "The change which our devotions are intended to make is upon ourselves, not upon the Almighty. Their chief efficacy is derived from the good dispositions which they raise and cherish in the human soul," &c. So Lord Kames writes: "The Being that made the world governs it by laws that are inflexible, because they are the best; and to imagine that he can be moved by prayers, oblations, or sacrifices to vary his plan of government, is an impious thought, degrading the Deity to a level with ourselves." His reason for prayer is, that it cultivates, by exercise, a devout habit of mind, and tends to purify it. Now there is nothing untrue in any of these statements in what they assert. It is true that prayer itself exercises a wholesome influence on the mind. He who prays opens his heart to God, and so is made ready to receive spiritual influences. But to make ourselves ready and fit to receive an influence is a different thing from giving this influence to ourselves. Prayer opens the heart to God; and when the heart is open, God will come in. But the opening of the door is one thing, and the entrance of the guest another.

One objection to this view of Prayer is, that it was not that of Jesus. His language plainly teaches, not that by assuming the attitude of prayer we shall magnetize our own mind, but that, if we pray, God will give, in consequence of our prayer, that which he would not give, or might not give, otherwise. And it is a very different thing, as regards the character of the prayer itself, which of these views we adopt. If we take the view of Jesus, we shall feel ourselves really in the presence of God, and shall be expecting to receive an influence from Him in our soul. If we adopt the other view, we shall feel that we are alone with ourselves, and shall be endeavoring to exert a beneficial influence on our own minds.

I think it is evident, that, with this view of Prayer, the tendency would be to discontinue it. Sincere and truthful men would find it hard to assume the appearance of asking God for that which, in reality, they expected to procure for themselves. They would find, or feel, a certain insincerity in such a course. The natural method with such a view of self-improvement would be meditation rather than prayer. We believe that, wherever these views have prevailed, they have had such an influence. Men holding such views may indeed continue to pray from the natural instinct of the human heart, but all that energy will be taken out of prayer which comes from belief in its real efficiency to obtain from God what we need.

This theory of Prayer is founded by the writers above quoted on two ideas. First, that prayer cannot produce any effect upon God; and second, that it cannot induce him to change his plans. But what reason have we to say that prayer cannot affect God. Is the Divine nature such that it is destitute of sympathy, or does the perfection of God consist in not being moved to feeling by the earnest cry of his child? Such is not the view given in the New Testament of the Deity, and there is no reason to doubt that the Divine nature, in its infinite grandeur and glory, is not cold or insusceptible, but, far more than ours, is capable of being moved by the emotions even of the lowest of his creatures. As regards the other idea, it is true that our prayers will not induce God to change his plans; but it may be a part of his plan to give us when we ask that which he would not otherwise bestow. And if this be a part of God's plan, then his immutability requires that he should change his course of conduct towards us because we pray. He adheres to his plan, by yielding to our prayer.

§ 23. *Prayer should be only for Spiritual Blessings.—Objections to this View.*

The other theory of Prayer, which many have adopted to escape supposed difficulties, is that which makes it proper only to ask for spiritual blessings, and not for temporal. Or, if we ask at all for temporal things, for outward mercies for ourselves or others, it should be, according to this theory, in the most general terms, and not with the expectation of really obtaining them by means of our prayer. This view is supported by many considerations. It is said that Jesus, where he promises that if we ask we shall receive, is speaking of the gift of the Holy Spirit,—that is, of spiritual blessings, and not of temporal. It is urged that we may ask in faith for purity, for love, for strength to resist evil, because we know that these are good for us, but that we cannot know, in regard to any temporal blessing, whether it is really a blessing or not. It is argued, that to ask God for outward things is a selfish and therefore not a Christian prayer, and that it is opposed to that trust in God which Jesus enjoins, when he says, "Take no thought for your life what ye shall eat, nor yet for your body what ye shall put on; for your Father knoweth that ye have need of these things." It is also argued that such a view of Prayer is too calculating, and not sufficiently spontaneous.

To these objections we reply, that, though Jesus speaks of the Holy Spirit in Luke xi. 13, he uses a more general expression in Matt. vii. 11, and that he both taught and showed, by his own example, at other times, that it was right also to pray for temporal needs. The Apostles sought help from God, and found it, in their outward necessities, and taught, even when laying the most stress upon works, that prayer also for the sick would effect their cure. It is true that we never can be sure that it is best for us to receive any temporal enjoyment, and therefore we ought always to pray, as Jesus prayed, submissively; asking that God's will, and not our will, should be done. But we see by the example of Jesus in the Garden, that a submissive prayer for outward things may be also a very earnest prayer. It may be that it would be an injury to us, and not an advantage, to obtain that for which we ask, and then if we ask in submission to God's wisdom and will, we shall not be cursed with an answered prayer. But it may be, on the other hand, that what we ask for is something that it would be really good for us to receive in answer to prayer, — something which God means that we should obtain by praying, — something which, thus obtained, will bring the soul nearer to him by its gratitude. So that there is danger on both sides; on one side danger of asking for something which we ought not to have, on the other side, danger of not receiving what would be good for us because we omit to ask for it. As the Apostle says, "Ye have not because ye ask not." (James iv. 2.) The only way of escaping both dangers is by asking earnestly, but submissively, for every thing which we think we need. And perhaps we may say, that we cannot be always certain that it is best for us to receive any particular spiritual blessing. Law, in his "Spirit of Prayer," has a fine passage, in which he argues that, though raptures of piety are often good for the soul, seasons of coldness and spiritual desolation may also be often good, and even better for the soul than the other, as producing a more entire dependence on God than could otherwise be obtained. The same thing also may be intended by the Apostle where he speaks of some temptation in the flesh (Gal. iv. 14), which seems to have been the evil from which he prayed thrice to be delivered, but had the answer, that God's strength was made perfect in his weakness. Therefore, if the fact that we know not whether any outward event may be really good for us to receive is a reason for not asking, the same reason may be urged against asking for any particular spiritual thing. As regards the selfishness of such prayers, we may reply, that it is certainly wrong to ask either for temporal or spiritual things selfishly; and as wrong in the latter case as in the former. To pray simply for our own sake to be saved from spiritual evil, is no more a Christian prayer, than to pray in the same manner to be saved from temporal evil. In both cases, the prayer beginning with the selfish need rises above it and goes beyond it. It asks for spiritual or for temporal good, for health of soul or health of body, in order to use them in the service of Christ and of man. And in both cases the prayer has the effect of lifting us out of that selfishness from which it began. And therefore we are not more selfish because we express these desires and needs to God, but less so. The selfish desire we have. The question is, whether we shall let it remain in the soul as a selfish wish, or, by expressing it to God, have it changed into a Christian, that is, a generous prayer. The objection, that to pray for temporal things is inconsistent with the command of Christ to take no thought concerning them because God knows that we have need of all these things, falls to the ground when we look at the meaning and reason of this command. The meaning is, that we are not to be anxious concerning outward things. And this is also true of spiritual things; for anxiety is as injurious in the one case as in the other. The command is to trust in God, and certainly Christianity requires us to trust in God with regard to the needs of the soul, no less than with regard to the needs of the body. The reason given is, that our Father knows that we have need of all these things; and certainly he knows also that we have need of spiritual things. This command, therefore, cannot establish a distinction between outward and inward blessings, so as to make it proper to pray for these, and not for those. And as regards the other objection, that Prayer would become a matter of calculation, and that this view is a utilitarian view, making it a contrivance for obtaining what we want, we would reply only, that, as a matter of necessity, a large part of life must belong to the sphere of prudence, if another part belongs to that of spontaneity ; and that therefore the question merely is whether this calculating part of life shall or shall not be excluded from the domain of Prayer.

Here, in fact, is the reason of prayer for temporal things. A large part of our life is necessarily occupied with them. God has made it so, and it is right that it should be so. He has so made us that we should be filled with an ardent interest in the persons and the events which surround us in life. He has enjoined no stoical indifference in regard to them. The Earth, full of beauty, full of wonder, was meant to interest the human soul, and draw out its faculties. Society, friendship, and love, all family affections, all social and national interests, were divinely bestowed upon man. Since, therefore, God has so made us that we must feel interested in these things, and means that we shall be interested in them, the question is, Shall we bring these interests to him or not? Shall we ask his sympathy and help in regard to them, or not. If not, then how large a part of the love, the wish, the purpose of the soul, which is its life, is shut out from God! How much of life is thereby desecrated and made unchristian! This view of Prayer is, in fact, only the reappearance in a new form of that idea of Christianity which divorced it from life, making one holy and the other profane. It is the same pernicious view which has taken religion out of week-days and confined it to Sundays, — out of the shop and street and shut it in the church, — out of the world of acting, loving, suffering man, and placed it in the small conventicle, the narrow sect. But Christ, when on earth, utterly discountenanced this view. He was present then at the marriage-feast, at the house of the publican, conversing with the sinners, and why not now? Then they prayed to him for help in outward, temporal necessities, and why not ask help in the same necessities now? Then he praised the faith of those who asked such temporal aid. Was it praiseworthy then to believe that the Divine Power would be exerted to cure disease, and is it wrong to believe it now? While answering such prayers and meeting such necessities of the present life, Jesus raised the thoughts of those whom he helped to higher necessities and higher blessings, and would not a like result obtain still?

CHAPTER IV.

PREPARATIONS FOR PRAYER.

§ 24. *General Remarks.*

HAVING thus considered the doctrine of the New Testament concerning Prayer, and examined the chief difficulties and objections, we pass on to consider the conditions and helps. Mental difficulties having been removed, moral difficulties present themselves, lying, perhaps, far deeper. For the moral preparation for prayer is more important than the intellectual preparation, and after all intellectual difficulties have been removed, greater difficulties may remain, arising from the state of the heart and the purposes. For it is evident that, if the prayer is to be any thing more than an outward form, it must be the expression of some real want. Every one knows that to say our prayers is not to pray; that words without thoughts never to heaven go. But it is not as often understood, that thoughts without affections are equally far from constituting a true prayer. We are very apt to confound an intellectual approbation of goodness with the desire for goodness. We ask for that which our conscience and moral sense teach us that we ought to pray for, and are satisfied with this, as though we had really prayed. But it is one thing to see what we ought to wish, and another thing to wish for it. To confound the two is to mistake the preparation of prayer for prayer itself. To meditate upon our wants, our sins, our occasions of gratitude, is a very good preparation for prayer, but it is not till meditation becomes affection that prayer really begins. But there is a still more subtle self-deception, which needs to be guarded against. We are often in danger of mistaking sentimental prayer for the prayer of conviction, faith, and love. There is in man a natural sentiment of religion, a feeling of reverence, which is more or less easily roused according to his organization. This also forms a good preparation for prayer and for the religious life. But these sentiments will not, by themselves, constitute Christian prayer. They are too much on the surface of the mind. They are too much mere emotion. They do not permanently connect themselves with the character. The true prayer, as we have seen, the only real Christian prayer, the only efficient prayer, the only prayer worth praying, is not the prayer of form, but of faith; not the prayer of the intellect, but of the heart; not flowing from a transient emotion, but from a permanent purpose; not originating in the sentiment of veneration, but in the Christian aim of life. How important, then, for true prayer is its preparation, and especially its moral preparation. All the difficulty lies here. The preparation for prayer being made, prayer itself comes spontaneously. No one need ever try to pray, for prayer is a free movement of the soul; but we may and must exert ourselves in making the moral preparation, and removing the moral obstacles in the way of prayer. Therefore, meditation and self-examination are always requisite as helps to prayer. The object of self-examination is to test our purposes and our desires; to see where we are and which way we are going, to deepen our convictions in regard to the presence of God and the eternal world. And more particularly as we have seen that three things are necessary to Christian prayer, — spirit, truth, and faith, — it is the object of our meditation to prepare ourselves as regards each of these essential elements of prayer.

§ 25. *Organic and Psychologic Preparations.*

Some years since, when the writer of this essay resided in a Western city, a distinguished Phrenologist visited the place, and made an examination of the heads of six Protestant clergymen. He pronounced them all deficient in the organ of Reverence or Veneration, said they had no devotional tendencies by nature, and added, that they ought not, any of them, to have become clergymen. And, what is more remarkable, all of these six clergymen admitted the correctness of his observation. They all declared it to be true that they had no special devotional or religious tendencies by nature, and that their religion had come to them, not in the way of development, but in that of crisis. As one of these clergymen, however, while admitting the fact as regarded myself, I denied the inference. For I believed that a person might be as well fitted for the office of a clergyman, whose religion was a matter of experience and conviction, — born out of the struggles of life, out of self-conflict and earnest endeavor, — as if it had grown up out of a large organic tendency. More so, perhaps; for such a man would be better qualified to meet the needs of others, who had felt in himself, in distinct throes of consciousness, the birth of the religious life, than if it had come to him as a special gift of nature.

Nevertheless, it is certain that there are organic and psychological preparations for prayer, which differ in every individual. Over these he has no power, and for the possession or absence of these he is not responsible. It is desirable that this should be understood, for many persons torment themselves needlessly, because they do not find in themselves the same devotional tendencies which they observe in others. On the other hand, those in whom the devotional sentiment is in surplus by natural endowment may be contented to rest therein, and so make of prayer a purely sentimental exercise and enjoyment. To avoid these errors, we must learn to distinguish between the glow of the organic tendency, the warmth of the sentiment, on one hand, and the earnestness which is given to prayer by conviction, purpose, and the stress of life. The organic tendency is a beautiful one, and if we possess it largely, is one for which we ought to be profoundly grateful. It leads us to look upward toward that which is above us, — leads us to reverence parents, superiors, heroes, saints, men of genius and greatness, men of virtue, —

and finally to adore and worship the Most High, and to find happiness therein. This sentiment is the crown of the moral nature; it gives harmony to the whole character, — eliminates all that is abrupt, harsh, coarse, and low; by giving humility it gives dignity, for it is a law of nature that those who humble themselves are exalted. This sentiment causes one to take pleasure in prayer, especially in that part of prayer which consists in adoration. As those who have much of this exquisite sentiment enjoy the sight, thought, and presence of venerable men, — love to be with the old, the wise, the honorable, — so they love to be in the presence of God. A tone of fair humility, of beautiful up-looking, pervades their prayers. But this action of this sentiment does not constitute the essence of prayer, nor give its substance; it only makes at most its element and sphere. It is a preparation for prayer, — leading us to recognize gladly God's presence, and opening the soul to meet him. But we may be glad to be in a person's presence, when we have nothing to say to him. And if we have nothing to say to him, we cannot have communion with him, — there is no real intercourse. We may talk to him, and look at him, and love to contemplate his face, and study his character; but this is only a preparation for intercourse, it is not intercourse itself. Some person who never saw him before, and who has not half the regard for him or respect which we have, may come to him on important business, and have a real intercourse with him, which we have never had.

It is necessary to understand this distinction between the prayer of natural sentiment, and the prayer of conviction, in order that those who are deficient in this beautiful tendency may not be discouraged thereby, and those who possess it not unduly self-satisfied. If we are thus endowed, we may be thankful for the gift, and find it a preparation for intercourse with the Heavenly Father. But if we are not thus endowed, it does not follow that we cannot pray, nor even that we cannot pray with depth and power. Conviction, purpose, a right direction of heart and life, will make our prayers genuine and joyful; though the natural sensibility which we observe in others is wanting.

But there are other organic faculties beside this tendency to adoration and reverence, which make a preparation for prayer. There are also tendencies to Hope and to Fear, the sense of Beauty and of Rectitude, and perhaps other powers and sensibilities which belong to the original endowments of the individual. When these, or either of these, are in large proportion, we can easily trace their influence in the devotional character. Hope gives confidence to prayer, causes it to rise joyfully to heaven. Fear makes prayer more urgent, more clinging and persevering. The sense of Beauty gives elevation and a picturesque coloring to the petitions and utterances. Conscientiousness makes the tone of confession more profound and sincere, makes the dedication of self to the will of God more earnest. Thus variously does Nature prepare us for entering the world of higher truth, and so does she prophesy, in her sure instincts, the food which is to be given to supply them. Only let us not mistake the instinct and tendency for its completion, the prophecy for its fulfilment.

Unquestionably all these faculties can be cultivated, they are all susceptible of education and improvement. But as no amount of education can make of some men great poets, orators, statesmen, — as no amount of culture can communicate to some persons a taste for science, mathematics, mechanics, — so to many persons no culture can convey the strong devotional tendencies which others inherit from nature. Let us be satisfied, therefore, that, beautiful as these tendencies are, they are not essential for communion with God; that, excellent as are these preparations of piety, there is another and "a more excellent way."

It is often said that woman is naturally more religious by nature than man. If Religion is here used in its large sense, as denoting our relations to God of love, trust, obedience, then the statement is manifestly untrue. At least it seems to us incredible, that the Deity should make such a distinction in the endowments of those who were intended to be helpmeets to each other in all things. But if it means that woman has a stronger tendency than man to the exercises of public worship, and finds more pleasure than man in adoration, there is no doubt that the statement is correct. The beautiful faculty of Reverence is more native to woman than to man. And for this endowment she may well be grateful, and, understanding its limitations, use it for her own elevation and that of her companion and children.

§ 26. *Preparation of the Heart.*

Let us now pass on to more important parts of the preparations of Prayer. These are of the Heart, Mind, and Will. In all these there is needed a general and a special preparation. We need, in general, to have the right Love, Belief, and Purpose, embodied in the tenor of our life, in order to pray aright. But as the cares and pleasures and occupations of the world confuse and dim these fundamental convictions and desires, they need to be refreshed by special effort, in order that our daily prayers may flow up out of the true fountains.

First, therefore, of the Preparation of Heart. It is clear that we cannot ask for any thing earnestly except we wish for it, — and that therefore except we are in our heart loving and seeking for spiritual things, we cannot sincerely ask for them. This is the truth in the apparently harsh doctrine that the prayers of the unregenerate are of no avail, and that an unconverted person has no right to pray. False as the doctrine is in this form, it involves a truth, — namely, that to pray to any good purpose, the general wish and desire of our soul must be for goodness. For in the first place, the main objects of Christian supplication and thanksgiving are spiritual blessings, and if we do not love them, we can be sincere neither in asking for them nor in returning thanks for them. And again, when asking for temporal blessings, we cannot ask for them in faith, unless we ask in a Christian spirit. So that he only can pray heartily, whose heart is right with God,—who is, in the deepest tendency of his hidden life, longing to know and love and serve God, as his main joy. The first preparation for prayer is to have this deep inner life of love. Out of this life, gratitude, supplication, confession, easily flow. The tendency of the soul being upward, the thoughts ascend easily, by their proper motion toward heaven, whenever the events of daily life supply the occasion. But where this tendency does not exist, there is always an effort required for prayer. In the one case the thoughts, like Milton's angels, tend naturally upward, by a specific levity, and descent or fall to them is adverse. In the other case, they tend downward by a specific gravity, toward the earthly end, the personal gratification, the egotistical triumph.

But supposing the main purpose and aim of life to be directed toward truth and right, the main current of the heart to be setting toward God and heaven, still it will happen that there will be eddies here and there running the other way. Often it will happen that we shall find ourselves for the time estranged from God, and then we shall often make the discovery of our estrangement by its effect upon our prayers. We find it difficult to pray, — we have nothing to say, — we pray from our memory of past needs, rather than from a sense of present ones. Our words mount up, our thoughts remain below. This state of mind indicates the estrangement of our heart from God, and warns us to return. Then a special preparation becomes necessary. We pray God to teach us how to pray. We reflect on our real needs till the desire for pardon, peace, the restoration of inward life, returns. We examine our past thoughts and actions till we discover what it is which has led us away from the true path. And so out of a genuine humility there springs up once more a sincere desire, and our prayer again becomes an utterance of the heart.

§ 27. *Preparation of the Mind.*

The mental preparation for prayer is given by the Apostle when he says, that "they who come to God must believe that he is, and that he is the rewarder of all those who diligently seek him." To pray, we must not only *wish* for what we pray, but believe that there is One who will give it in consequence of our asking. The former part of this essay has been intended to produce this conviction. But still special mental preparations are often necessary before the act of prayer, — a collecting of our thoughts, a consideration of our needs, a meditation on our circumstances.

First, consider the importance of preparation.

Prayer is the highest act of the human soul, the most sublime moment in human life, the most wonderful privilege of man. It certainly gives a singular dignity to "the awful soul which dwells in clay," it certainly tends to destroy the vain distinctions of our outward life, and to inspire us with a just respect for the meanest of our fellow-creatures, to know that this high privilege belongs to all. That forlorn wretch, who has no human friend, may dwell in intimate friendship with the Sovereign of the world, — that ignorant mind, in helpless darkness as regards all earthly knowledge, may possess himself of the highest idea in the universe, — that sinner, whom even good men shrink from, may commune intimately with the All-Holy, the All-Glorious. But in proportion to the greatness and blessedness of this privilege, its perversion is the more deplorable. There is nothing in the world more ineffably blessed and sublime than true prayer. But when prayer becomes a form, a ceremony, a cold task, a decency, an external duty, it is the most offensive of human falsehoods. Mock not God, de grade not yourselves, by such prayers as these. A prayer which is felt to be merely a form comes over the soul of the sincere man like a freezing blast from a sea of ice. We wish to stop our ears and flee away from it.

Prayer is approaching voluntarily the Holiest and Loftiest Being. You would not run heedlessly into the presence of an eminent person, — you would not go to visit a great or good man without some consideration of what you should say to him. You would wish to dress your mind in its best thoughts, to lay before him your choicest and most valued knowledge; you would wish to be in a calm, and true, and gentle mood. Is not equal reverence due to God? Prayer also is a great action. It requires energy to pray. It requires us to concentrate and direct our mind toward the Unseen, the Spiritual, the Infinite; and with earnest effort to carry up our thoughts, our needs, our love. But how often we pray without any such preparation, because the usual time for prayer has arrived? Such prayers must very often be false and hollow, made up of words of wind. If we were always in a spiritual frame, no preparation would be necessary. But until we attain that spiritual state, until we become perfect men in Christ Jesus, until our whole life becomes a prayer and a psalm, we should make a preparation, if only for a few moments, before every prayer. We should turn in, and examine our state of mind, and see whether we are ready to perform this high act.

Next consider the nature of this preparation.

It should consist, first, *in realizing the presence of God.* "He that cometh to God must believe that *he is*," — and that not merely in the cold and heartless assent of the intellect to the theological assertion that there is a First Cause. No. But if your mind has been separated from God by low cares, by worldly labors, if you have lost the sense of his great Presence, — turn in, — realize now where you are, who is near you, whose eye is upon you. That ever open eye, to whose glance the night shineth as the day, that dread Presence which walks unseen on our right hand and our left, that awful and Infinite Being who holds us in the hollow of his hand, — realize that He is very nigh thee, — not afar off upon some distant throne, but giving thee the very breath which speaks his praise, moving the very pulse which throbs in warm gratitude to him, the life of thy life. Thus let thy words not be sent forth into a void inane to search for a distant Power, but breathed reverently to Him who knows the unuttered thought.

Then, when we realize that we are in God's presence, let us also realize *why* we pray, what we need, — let us understand ourselves. Perhaps it is the close of the day. It has been a day of toil and of care; but now we are at its close, — the world is shut out, and we are alone with hearts which beat in warm sympathy with our own. We are about to thank God; but let us see first whether we are ready to thank him with our hearts. Are we really sensible of the love which has attended us through the day? are we sensible that it was *God's* love which welcomed us in the cheerful morning from the fresh air and the bright sky, — that it was *God's* love which shone upon us from the kind eyes of earthly affection, or when in a friend's words, in a book which we opened for a moment, a thought came to us of high and generous virtue, which inspired us for the moment with a breathing after the same? We were in a gloomy mood, dispirited and sad, and a letter was brought to us, the words of which lay warm at our heart for hours. In all these events, and a thousand like events, do we stop with the earthly cause, or have we penetrated through to the Heavenly Cause? If we have seen God in these gifts, then we shall thank him sincerely now. So, too, in our prayer we are about to confess our sins. But, first, let us be sure that we *feel* our sins. Do we think how, all through this day, our feelings have been morose, our temper fretful, our words harsh and unkind so that on the whole we have been making all around us unhappy rather than increasing their joy? Do we remember that we missed opportunities to-day, through our selfishness or indolence, of doing actions which would have made others happier or better, — opportunities which we shall never have again? Do we remember how our proud, careless words have led others to make light of sin, — have weakened their principles? Do we remember having acted the part of Satan to any, tempting them to evil instead of strengthening them for good? Do we remember how our duties, even when done, have been done with the hand rather than the heart, coldly and mechanically? Do we remember all the careless words we have spoken, some of which were barbed arrows of unkind surmise, of harsh and cruel judgment? It was our duty this day to have loved God with all our mind, heart, soul, and strength, and our neighbor as ourself. Alas! where has our love been? Perhaps we have not thought of God at all. Perhaps we have only thought of our neighbor to use him for our profit, to sneer at his character, to wound his feelings.

I think if we ask ourselves such questions as these, that we shall be able to say with sincerity in our prayer, "God be merciful to me a sinner!"

And then, also, we propose to ask God to deliver us from evil and make us pure and holy. But let us be sure that we really wish to be delivered from evil, that we are really conscious of the guilt and woe of sin, that we are deeply submissive to the will of God, and are ready to have him do with us what he will. If we have no strong desire for redemption, no hunger and thirst after righteousness, no purpose of self-consecration and submission, it is worse than vain to utter the *words* of petition. Let us then realize how much we need Divine help and the spirit of God in our hearts to form them anew into the image of his Son. Let us look forward to the duties which lie before us, to the judgment which is to come, to the accountabilities we are under. Judging by the past, we may see how unfit we are to meet these duties and responsibilities, how certainly we shall always fail in the hour of temptation, as we always *have* fallen, unless God shall create in us a new heart, inspire us with a deeper faith, stronger convictions of the danger and guilt of sin, and a more solemn sense of eternal realities. Such reflections as these will make us in earnest, when we ask Divine help and succor.

§ 28. *Experience. — Out of the Depths.*

A further preparation may come to us out of the deeper experiences of life. We may pray sincerely, but superficially, from the surface rather than from the depths of the mind. We may pray from our perception of what is right and true, rather than from a deep feeling of it. But when we can say with the Psalmist, "*Out of the* DEPTHS have I cried unto thee, O God!" then we have achieved also the moral preparation for prayer, the preparation of a moral experience. Then we acquire the habit of prayer out of *the deep places* of life, and the deep places of the heart.

There are *deep places in life.* For years we pass on in a circle of routine, until we reach a crisis. Sometimes years of cloudless prosperity are at once interrupted by a succession of troubles, as the smooth stream of a river is broken by rapids and hurried suddenly down a cataract. The happy family is entered by Death, — father, mother, children, are snatched away from that loving circle. Love is disappointed, — hopes are frustrated, — prosperity ceases, — adversity comes, — sickness despoils us of our energies. In such hours we seem to descend, step by step, into still more profound depths of trial and sorrow. But from these depths the heart sees God more clearly than from the sunny hill-tops of a happy life, — as persons can see the stars at midday from the bottom of a well. When all around us grows dark, the inward light grows stronger and clearer. When man deceives us, God is faithful. When Death approaches us outwardly, the idea of Immortal Life dawns, in pure auroral light, within the heart. In such hours we learn to pray.

But there are deeps lower than those of trouble and outward affliction, — moments in which, though no external trouble comes near us, inward joy departs. There are depths of scepticism which the soul of man has sometimes to pass, in his pilgrim's progress toward God, — depths in which we lose our faith in God, in man, in ourselves, — in which we ask for the meaning of the world, and find none, — in which all things seem full of vanity and emptiness, and we cause our heart to despair of all its labor which it takes under the sun. Blacker than

Egyptian darkness is this mental gloom, which sometimes settles, for a time, upon the purest and most aspiring minds, —

> " A grief without a pang, void, dark, and drear,
> A stifled, drowsy, unimpassioned grief,
> Which finds no natural outlet, no relief
> In word, or sigh, or tear."

In this condition of scepticism, when we are like children lost in a forest, what can we do but cry to God? This is the remedy, this the cure. It is not reasoning or argument which can help us in this disease, but Prayer. If we have faith enough left to cry to God, Peace and Light may then return to us.

But below this depth there is yet another, — the depth of Sin. What a terrible moment is that which reveals to us our sins, — which shows us how we have been selfish and ungrateful, proud and vain, worldly and frivolous! Sometimes the veil seems to be taken from our heart, and a mirror put before it, and we see our own wilfulness and selfishness. There they pass before us, in long procession, our vanished years; each turning upon us a sad, reproachful face, as though it said, " Why did you lose *my* golden opportunities? why fill my hours with thoughtless folly? why suffer me to be stained with evil thought and action?" The sin which, when we committed it, we excused so easily, and thought so lightly of, now stands before us dark and terrible. Conscious of our degradation, of our lost innocence, of our chilled affections and debased purposes, what can we do, in this moment of remorse, but *cry unto God?* Out of this deep too we may cry, and be heard. He who stood afar off, and smote upon his breast, saying, "God be merciful to me, a sinner!" — he went down to his house justified, rather than the other.

But if there are these depths of sorrow, there are deep places of joy also along our pathway, — when life becomes suddenly rich and full and hopeful, — when all within and around smiles. As sometimes, after a cold and backward spring, one warm week will open all the buds and dress the trees with blossoms, and fill the air with fragrance wafted from a thousand flowers, — so sometimes in life. The mother clasps her new-born infant to her heart, and her heart grows even more full of gratitude to God than of love to her child. The darling sister or daughter is restored to us from the bed which seemed that of death; or there comes to us an inward light, — we are lifted from misty doubt into clear convictions, — our path of life is made clear to us. We see what we ought to do, and God nerves us with strength to do it. We are equal to the hour which demands a sacrifice for principle. Conscience is obeyed, and in the calm tranquillity which follows we have a foretaste of heaven. We see the dawning of truths intended to be the "master lights of all our being," — we see the beauty of holiness, of purity, of generosity, of heroic self-denial, — and humbling ourselves as little children before them, we are rewarded with a child's joy.

Such are some of the *Deep Moments of Life*, out of which if we cry to God, our prayer is not one of form, thought, and sentiment merely, but of sincerity and truth. Such moments will lead us to understand ourselves, will lead us inward, will deepen our characters, and make our common prayers to flow, not from the surface but from the *Deep Places of the Mind.*

For we are complex beings. There is much on the surface of our soul, and many things below it. But the real prayer is that which comes from below, — out of the depths. And while the surface of the soul says one thing, its depth may say quite another. But the true prayer is the deep prayer.

There is a deep place of love in the heart of

man, — there is a deep current of affection which is his real life. Wherever that flows, there goes he. Wherever that tends, that is his tendency. He may have other desires, different from this main desire, inconsistent with it, opposed to it, perhaps, but these are only transient and ineffective wishes; this is the constant and controlling will. These are the *eddies* only; this, the *current*.

So, too, there is a deep *Thought* and a superficial *Thought*. The deep thought is our real, abiding conviction; the superficial thought is our present belief, our transient opinion. In many men, what they call their belief is only what they think they believe, or think they ought to believe, or would like to believe. It does not stand rooted in their experience, fastened to the mind by the results of observation, trial, reflection. They do not believe, but, as has been well said, they only make believe. Now what sort of a prayer is that which comes from such superficial affections and opinions? It is no real prayer. With his superficial thoughts and wishes, a man prays to God for piety, truth, and goodness, for virtue and heaven. But meantime, with his inmost will, with his deepest conviction, he prays for wealth, triumphs, honors, popularity. In these he really believes, for these he really longs. This, then, is his real prayer.

Especially a man prays well who prays out of the depths of his actual life. That which we are living for, that we can easily pray for. If we are living towards generous and humane ends; if we are living to advance a little the upward progress of humanity, to remove a little the crushing burdens which rest on human hearts; if we are living to do good to others and become better ourselves, — O, how easily shall we pray out of such a life as this! As naturally as smoke ascends to lose itself and become pure in the upper regions of the air, will our anxious and troubled thoughts rise to God, and find themselves calmed and strengthened in his presence. Then we shall not be divided, distracted, uncertain. We shall pray our work, and act out our prayers. Our prayers will not be formal, forced, laborious, but simply the walking before God, walking in his spirit, and continuing to receive light, love, and strength from him. Thus shall we call upon God evermore out of the depths of life and out of the depths of the mind.

CHAPTER V.

METHODS.

§ 29. *Private Prayer.*

THE largest part of the Christian's prayers will always be private. His prayers will be a dialogue with his Heavenly Father. If his religion is not so, he may distrust its sincerity. If it be not more secret than public, more hidden than open, — if his prayers in his closet, in his studies, in his walks, are not far more constant and important than his prayers in company and in church, — he ought to doubt whether he does not pray to be seen of men rather than to be seen and heard of God. Secret prayer is the fountain of all other prayer. Where there is no habit of private communion with God, there will be no earnestness in public prayer. It will be formal, dry, and consisting in endless repetitions of the customary phrases. The life of religion in the soul consists in habitual communion with God, in gratitude, in supplication, in " the flight of one alone to the Only One." This hidden, inner life must be maintained in its fulness by constant prayer, and thus it will flow out easily into all the acts of public devotion and active goodness. But when this inner life stagnates, then the outward acts of devotion become formal and rigid, and the man is like a tree, hollow at heart, which still may maintain an outward languid show of life; or like an olive-tree dead at the root, which still may bear "two or three berries in the top of the uppermost bough, four or five in the outmost fruitful branches thereof."

Secret Prayer is the sign and the food of this inner life. Its sign, — for this life is love, and where love exists, it will express itself. If the heart loves God, it will commune with him, it will habitually turn to him, as the heliotrope to the king of day; it will lean on him in dependence, trust, and confidence. Its food, — for such communion opens the soul to receive new life flowing into it from God, and prayer is the door through which the bread and wine of the soul are brought in.

One great advantage of Private or Individual Prayer is its freedom of form; another, its greater range of subjects and occasions. Its form is free. It may be mental or oral, it may be only the unexpressed, sincere desire of the soul, or it may be a verbal utterance of wants and needs. It may be

> "The burden of a sigh,
> The falling of a tear,
> The upward glancing of an eye,
> When none but God is near," —

or it may be a written form of self-dedication, carefully prepared, and solemnly read once and again on the bended knees. It may be at set times or at any and every time, — walking to and fro, sitting, kneeling, waking at midnight on the bed, in the midst of affairs. We carry this closet with us everywhere, we can always step in and shut the door. No one sees that we have gone in, unless our secret communion with our Father shows itself by "a sweet, attractive kind of grace," which such intercourse leaves behind it on the features.

Sometimes the deepest prayer of all is not only without utterance, not only without words, but even goes down below the region of distinct thought. It is simply turning to God, and opening the heart to him, to receive whatever influence he may send. It is the state of mind described in all the Quaker books of devotion, and expressed in the sweet Methodist hymn, which seems written not for Methodists, but to be sung in the Friends' meeting-house: —

> "From the world of sin and noise
> And hurry I withdraw;
> For the small and inner voice
> I wait with silent awe;
> Silent am I now and still,
> Dare not in thy presence move:
> To my waiting soul reveal
> The secret of thy love."

And as the form of Secret Prayer is thus free, so are its topics extensive. Every thing furnishes occasions and subjects for Private Prayer. Things which we could not mention before men we can express to God. Thoughts too private and intimate, facts too familiar, needs of the day and hour, all circumstances which befall us, all occasions which we have to encounter, all dangers and temptations which we may foresee impending, all opportunities of usefulness which we may anticipate, — these all may furnish themes and incitements to devotion. The minister going to visit a parishioner, the lawyer rising to plead a cause, the physician entering the sick-room, the mechanic engaging in daily labor, the teacher, the shopkeeper, and any one, of whatever occupation, may all turn in first, to ask a heavenly aid for the earthly task. We are about to go among friends, or among strangers, and our words may do them good, may do them harm; shall we not ask that our words may be rightly guided? We are likely to meet temptations, — temptations to vary a little way from strict honesty, strict truth, strict purity; we are tempted to doubt, to despair, to weariness; we are tempted to take a dark view of life, of human nature; — let us pray! We are to be placed among opponents, enemies; we shall be tempted to return railing for railing, evil for evil; — let us pray! Thus arise around us the manifold occasions for private prayer, — for a word, a thought, a longing. Things which could not well be said in the presence of others, may be expressed in these moments of intimate, interior communion.

§ 30. *Family and Social Prayer.*

The first form of open prayer is in the family, and as soon as we pass from the sphere of private prayer into this, we lose much of the extent of topics and freedom of method. Family devotion is both important and difficult, — the difficulty arising from the fact, that the members of a family, having so much else in common, may not necessarily have the same religious life. This makes the selection of topics and their treatment a matter of no small importance. The topics should not be abstract and general, but local and particular; they should grow out of the family life, and the relations of parents and children, husband and wife, master and servant. As regards the method of family devotion, it may be recommended to have all the members of the household take part in it, by reading from the Scriptures in turn, by singing hymns in common, by responses and alternate oral utterance. For this purpose a devotional manual is desirable, and where this cannot be used, the reading in common of the devotional Psalms. In this way the service may not only be made less tedious, but a living interest may grow up in it; and years after, children may look back to the influences of these morning and evening hours, as sources of present strength and peace to their hearts.

The Social Prayer, where two or three unite together who are both intimate with each other and also disciples of the same Master and believers in the same truth, is something intermediate between Private and Public Prayer. It has something of the freedom and range of private prayer, and the added force of sympathy from the union of accordant minds. The small meetings of Christian friends in the parlor or vestry are often felt to bring the soul nearer to God than the worship of the great congregation, in which the diversity is too great to allow of a close union of thought. It is therefore a very useful practice in a church to hold meetings for conference and prayer, which will be always attended by those who are near together in sympathy. Such meetings warm the hearts, and kindle anew the fading flame of devotion. There is no reason why they should not be adopted by all sects; especially if they are adopted and retained, not as a decent form, but only while they are living, and filled with a living interest. The morning prayer-meeting, where Christian friends may meet for half an hour before engaging in the duties of the day, may be, as it has been, a source of strength to many for the common labors and trials of life.

§ 31. *Public Prayer.*

The subject of Public Worship is too large to be treated here with any fulness. I shall merely venture a few suggestions in relation to the two questions, "What are the reasons for maintaining Public Worship?" and, "How is this Public Worship to be made most interesting and useful?"

Public worship has this great advantage and value, — that it recognizes a public religious sentiment. It is a perpetual denial by the Christian Church of its own doctrine of Total Depravity. It assumes that the whole community, the converted and the unconverted, the regenerate and the unregenerate, *can* pray, *ought* to pray, *wish* to pray. It so far counteracts the pharisaic feeling engendered by these distinctions. It is, moreover, a religious education for the whole community. Who can tell the amount of influence exerted, directly and indirectly, by the fact of Sunday worship pervading the whole land, of Sunday stillness, cessation from business, of church-bells, and the streets filling with the currents of piety which set toward the house of God? Who can estimate the impression made by the sight of young and old, rich and poor, all classes, all orders, equalized before God in a common worship, — by the great assembly kneeling together, responding together, lifting their voices with one accord in solemn hymns and anthems, moved by a common feeling and conviction in listening to the word read or spoken?

it is a humanizing influence, purifying and elevating the community, keeping alive the sense of God's presence in the world and nearness to the human heart, keeping up a Christian standard of duty and responsibility. The power of this institution of public worship as a means of Christian education can only be realized by those who have lived in those outskirts of civilization where it has not gone, and have seen the results of its first introduction. In the Western States of this Union, towns have grown up containing one thousand or fifteen hundred inhabitants, in which there has been no regular public worship. Such communities are without order or peace, — they are the abodes of violence, intemperance, and all forms of brutal vice. At last there comes some preacher of the Gospel, — a travelling Methodist, perhaps, with all his library contained in his saddle-bags, who composes his sermons while riding beneath the shade of the majestic forests of beech and tulip-tree, who finds his congregation of an evening in a country schoolhouse, or in the open woods, who combines in himself the functions of preacher, choir, and sexton, and whose only emolument is his supper and lodging. Such a man comes into the town, finds out and brings together those who are wishing for a more Christian society, establishes some regular public worship, and thus sets on foot a humanizing influence. A new public opinion is created, favorable to order, civility, and peace. In the course of a few years the aspect of affairs is wholly altered, the rudeness and violence are gone, and are replaced by habits of sobriety and decency. Now, in this case, the Church, with its institution of worship, does not act as a police, restraining the outbreak of crime, but as an educational influence, correcting the tendencies to crime. In this instance we have given the history of what has actually occurred again and again, in numberless instances throughout our Western States, within the last half-century.

But not only does public worship tend to educate the community by awakening and developing religious ideas, but it also cultivates humane feelings, brings the different classes of society near to each other, makes one common platform on which all can stand together, and so counteracts continually the tendencies to separate and isolated life. People who live all other days apart from each other, whose lives are narrowed to little rounds of domestic duty, who see only small family groups and cliques, come into church on the Lord's day, and feel themselves for an hour at one with all classes of men. This hour, though only bringing them into an external contact, and no intimate communion, does much to emancipate them from a narrow and too individual life. All professions, conditions, characters, are side by side engaged in the same serious occupation. Political opponents here forget their disputes, — rivals in fashion, competitors in business, rich and poor, are here brought into a certain sympathy ; — and this is no small gain.

We say no more here of the advantages of Public Worship, since this topic needs no special treatment, but pass on to the more important question, How shall it be made most interesting and useful ?

The interest of Public Worship depends chiefly on this, — that it shall be a *reality*, and not a *form*. If, when we enter the church, we are made to feel that we are among a people who have met only because it is a custom so to meet ; if there is no awe, no earnestness, no devotion, no humanity ; if we perceive the airs of fashion, display, egotism, self-conceit, in the attitudes, looks, and gestures of the assembly, — not only is there no good done, but there is a positively evil influence. We can bear these manifestations elsewhere, but not here ; — here they disgust and offend us, and make us doubt the reality of all faith and all religious feeling.

For it is no doubt the fact, that we feel at once what is the spirit of a congregation. Seriousness manifests itself inevitably without effort, in the attitudes, looks, gestures. Frivolity manifests itself as inevitably in careless attitudes, and gestures or looks which express indifference to others, satisfaction with self, irreverence toward God. You cannot enter a congregation without feeling at once this spirit, and you unconsciously sympathize with it. The voluntary on the organ tells you that the organist is wishing to show off his technical skill and power over the instrument; — the choir say in their singing, very audibly, "We are paid so much for coming here, and we must do this as a matter of business," or, "We wish to show you what fine voices we have, and what we are able to execute." The minister reads or prays, and the sound of his voice says, "I am unprepared to pray, — I have nothing of the spirit of prayer; but I am going to assume a solemn tone, so as to convince myself and you that I am quite in earnest." All this worldliness and indifference and languor passes into the congregation. As they repose in the corners of the pews, as they sit and stand and stare in all directions, with empty or supercilious gaze, they declare plainly that they have come to church with no religious interest or aim, and that they will probably leave it with no religious impression. The sermon is, in such cases, the only hope for the service. In *that* the minister is likely to be really interested, since he has written it with thought and care, and therefore he will more or less interest the congregation, and so some good will be done.

When worship is felt to have thus degenerated into a form, empty of meaning and life, serious persons will be revolted by it, and will be tempted to desert public worship altogether. Yet in so doing they will miss the advantages above mentioned, and will feel that they are becoming lonely and morbid in their interior life. Therefore the question is, How shall new life and earnestness be breathed into public worship, so as to make it really interesting and useful?

There are two ways in which this end may be reached. First, the minister and the congregation may make direct efforts to obtain a new and earnest interest in their worship, and secondly, they may indirectly seek it through the medium of new forms and improved methods. There are these two wants, — the want of New Wine and the want of New Bottles, — of a new spirit, and of new forms. A new spirit will give novelty and interest to old forms, and new forms will often awaken a new spirit.

Let the minister feel an earnest desire to give new life to the public worship, — let him never enter the pulpit without mental and moral preparation, — let him never engage in public prayer, until he has privately asked God's aid that he may pray in spirit and in truth, — let him revolve the needs of his congregation, feel a living sympathy with them all, the happy and the sorrowful, the believers and the doubters, the old and the young. Let him pray out of this depth of conviction, out of this fulness of interest, and the congregation will become more or less interested too. The spirit of religion is as contagious as that of indifference, and will pass into their hearts, and a new earnestness will manifest itself outwardly, which will tend to perpetuate, deepen, and extend the spirit. Earnest persons in the congregation will become more in earnest, there will be a real revival of the spirit of piety and faith, and, without changing a single method, every part of the service will be lifted out of deadness into life.

Or, on the other hand, something may be done

by introducing new forms. Any kind of a change, which breaks up old habits, which takes the congregation out of the stereotyped ways, may often tend to give new earnestness to the services. Innovations in either direction, whether toward more of Form, or more of Freedom, have produced a deeper life. The churches which have copied Roman Catholic customs, putting candles on the altar, and the like, have usually with their unimportant novelties gained an important increase of real religious interest. So, too, churches which have thrown away forms and simplified worship have been benefited. Not that the change in itself, and absolutely, was necessarily for the better, but by the change they were taken out of the grooves of form, and thrown upon the help of the spirit.

What these changes of method and form shall be, depends much on the character and circumstances of the society. They should not be introduced by a mere majority vote, against the wishes of a respectable minority, since the advantage gained would be more than counterbalanced by the feeling of dissatisfaction introduced into the congregation. Such changes may be made the subjects of interesting and useful discussion in the meetings of the society, and may be gradually introduced, according to their wishes.

We do not mean to say that one mode of worship has *no* absolute advantage over any other. We find something good in all, but some no doubt are really better and others worse. There are vicious extremes of too much of Form, running into formalism, — of too little, passing into disorder. We can conceive of a mode of worship which should combine the advantages of all others, — which should be neither bald in its simplicity, nor loaded with ornament and variety, — in which the congregation should take part orally as well as mentally, by congregational singing and responses, — which should be in part Liturgic and in part Extemporaneous, — in which there should be seasons of silence for mental prayer and contemplation, — and in which choral and instrumental music should be alternated with the hymns of the whole congregation. Such a worship might be aided by the construction of the building and its ornaments. The house should not be gloomy, but pervaded by a cheerful light, coming mostly from above. The seats should be arranged in a circular form, so as to bring the people into each other's view as well as into that of the minister, and so to make a visible communion. Paintings might be on the walls, representing the Parables of Christ, scenes in his life, and important events in Church history. Thus a truly catholic church architecture might be produced, equally distant from the baldness of Puritanism, and the gloom and closeness of the Roman churches. For we cannot believe that the mediæval architecture, beautiful as it was in its time, was intended for all time. The idea of humanity is lost sight of, the congregation are like ants crawling on the floor; only the altar and its mass, the priesthood and their ceremonies, are of consequence. The whole of Catholic worship consists in looking at the celebration of the Mass, — the whole of Puritan worship consists in listening to the prayers, hymns, and sermon. This *looking* and *listening* needs to be superseded by a higher worship, in which the church of brethren and sisters shall worship in communion with each other, and not vicariously by priest or preacher. Then the house of worship would not be only a floor beneath a lofty roof, where a congregation stands to see a mass, — nor pews in which they sit to hear a sermon. But the house of worship would be a home, and the worshippers therein a family, — and to make of the church a home is the surest way of making the home a church.

§ 32. *Liturgic or Extemporaneous.*

From what we have said it will be seen that we vote neither with the friends of a liturgy nor with their opponents in the much debated question concerning forms of prayer. We believe the best form of worship to be that which combines the two methods. It is well for the congregation to take part in the worship orally as well as mentally, for thus they m[illegible]tize each other by the sound of their voices, and the utterance reacts on themselves. But a liturgy which is fixed and unvarying, and which leaves no place for prayer adapted to varying circumstances and needs, becomes a routine and a formality to many minds. But to the combination suggested of the two methods, we can see no possible objection, and wherever it has been tried, it has been successful.

§ 33. *Stated Times and Spontaneous.*

The element of prayer is freedom; and accordingly it should be encouraged to utter itself in spontaneous expressions of desire gratitude, dependence, contrition, joy. The child should have that confidence in his Father, that he can naturally and easily say to Him whatever he wishes, without formal preparation. Wherever there is a true union between the soul and God, prayer will flow out freely and easily as the prattle of an infant at its mother's knee. It will not be restrained by fear, for there is no fear in love, nor constrained by conscience, for love is the fulfilment of all law, nor stiffened by a formal propriety, which has no place in the intercourse of confiding friendship. The best, highest prayers are always most spontaneous, and wherever the spirit of prayer is, the largest part of devotion must come rather from an impulse than a purpose. The child does not say, "Go to, I will make a speech to my father," — "Come now, it is time to tell my mother that I love her, and to ask her to take care of me to-day." There must be a fountain of confiding love in the heart, which easily flows out in prayer, or the vitality of devotion is wanting. The life of prayer, therefore, is spontaneity, and its essential element perfect freedom.

But though rules are not appropriate as restraint, they may be useful as aids. Prudent arrangements may come in as auxiliary to impulse. To pray at stated times, if done from constraint and as a matter of formal duty or propriety, is not well; but if done from a wise desire to regulate life to the best advantage, may be very useful. We merely mean to oppose the *opus operatum* view of prayer. We oppose the notion, that, when a person has *said* his prayers at the proper times, once, twice, or thrice per day, he has done his duty. This *opus operatum* view pervades all prayer, Protestant and Roman Catholic, but is most plainly taught in the latter form of Christian belief. It is for instance, a rule of the Roman Church that the priest shall read his Breviary or Prayer-book one hour and a half every day. Accordingly, you find the priests reading their books in the railroad-cars, in the *salles d'attente*, or wherever they may happen to find a spare minute, looking about meanwhile in a way which shows how much this practice has become a mere lip-service. And how, with such a rule, can it be any thing else? But that one should arrange life a little, and appoint himself a time for prayer is natural and useful, — just as two friends, who love each other's society, may appoint certain hours for meeting, and arrange their other duties so as to secure this opportunity. But if these two friends should adopt as an inflexible rule that they should talk together one hour and a half every day, the life of their intercourse would soon be gone.

It is therefore proper and useful to fix certain hours for prayer, and those who do not do this will not be likely to find time for prayer. Regularity is not necessarily formality. What these times shall be, depends on the circumstances of the individual. The morning and evening have always been regarded as the most suitable seasons, and it is quite an advantage if one can so arrange his life as to have some time at the beginning of the day to consider what lies before him of duty, temptation, social intercourse, and responsibility, and seek for God's guidance and help to meet the occasions of the day in a true spirit. And so, at the close of the day, he does well who never goes to sleep without first looking to God in thankfulness, penitence, and reliance,—who commits himself, his family, his friends, to that Great Guardian, before passing into the region of unconscious repose. And here we may be permitted to refresh ourselves and our readers with the familiar lines of Henry Ware.

"To prayer, to prayer! for the morning breaks,
And earth in her Maker's smile awakes;
His light is on all below and above,
The light of gladness, and life, and love.
O, then, on the breath of this early air,
Send upward the incense of grateful prayer!

"To prayer! for the glorious sun is gone,
And the gathering darkness of night comes on:
Like a curtain from God's kind hand it flows,
To shade the couch where his children repose.
Then kneel, while the watching stars are bright,
And give your last thoughts to the Guardian of night.

"Never forget, my boy, to say your prayers every day, morning and night," — these words, spoken to a young man about to leave his father's roof for the first time, we have known to prove his preservation amid the temptations of a subsequent career. Let then spontaneity be joined with regularity, — the one making prayer vital, the other making it habitual, — the one being its life, the other its form, — the one its soul, and the other its body. Let the family assemble regularly for morning or evening prayer, let a moment of silence or a word of thanksgiving precede the united meal. But let not spontaneous prayer be excluded nor thought indecorous in the household life. When the thoughts have gone into a deeper channel than usual, when the conversation has been on serious duty, danger, or work, — when the heart has expressed its sense of need, the mind its want of guidance, — then let it be considered natural and fit for friends to pray for each other, for a moment to be given to devotion. Would not such a conversation have a fitting end in a prayer, and would it not be very proper for one asked for counsel, or trusted with confidence, to say, at the close of the dialogue, "Shall I not pray with you, now, my friend?"

§ 34. *Without Ceasing.* (See § 13.)

Unceasing prayer, therefore, does not exclude stated prayer, but rather includes it. Out of its root, in a heart loving to dwell near to God, and a life ordered and regulated so as to continue near to him, prayer ascends and becomes the spirit which animates all thought, all emotion, all activity. Head, heart, and hand are guided by a sense of a divine presence and love, in the midst of all tasks and joys.

"The morning comes, with blushes overspread,
And I, new-wakened, find a morn within;
And in its modest dawn around me shed,
Thou hear'st the prayer and the ascending hymn."

Prayer "without ceasing" does not, of course, mean an unceasing act of conscious address to God, but it means a spirit turned habitually toward God, and not from him. Such a spirit will make it natural and easy to speak to God whenever occasion arises, — natural also *not* to speak when there is no occasion. It makes of his service perfect freedom. It makes us feel surrounded and upheld by everlasting arms. It is not only the result and crown of all other prayer, but its root and source. For it really would seem that we cannot pray at all, unless we pray without ceasing. The mind must be either alienated from God or at peace with him, — either turned from him or turned toward him. But a mind alienated from God cannot pray, does not feel able to pray, is conscious that, instead of a Father to speak to, there is only a void inane. On the other hand, a mind at one with God, and at peace with him, is always in the sunshine of his presence, and a deep sense of contact and communion with God pervades all of life, and is the root of all actual prayer. The current of our being sets that way, and carries all our thoughts easily upward into the Divine presence. The inmost language of the heart is, —

> "Nearer, my God, to Thee, — nearer to Thee, —
> Even though it be a cross which raiseth me."

And this unceasing prayer of the heart is unceasingly answered in the sense of progress, in the conviction that we

> "nightly pitch our moving tent
> A day's march nearer home."

Therefore, when the Apostle says, "Pray with

out ceasing, and in every thing give thanks," he is not setting forth some ultimate and almost impossible attainment of piety, which only is accomplished by here and there a saint, half-liberated from earth and sense. He is, as almost always, speaking to us all. Those who pray at all, to any purpose, pray without ceasing. All real Christians pray without ceasing. For our uttered and stated prayers are not isolated efforts of piety; not occasional returns, twice or thrice a day, out of worldliness into religion, out of atheism into devotion. But much rather are they the moments when the steady current of our inward and hidden life, flowing ever toward Truth and Goodness, is tossed up into waves and jets of conscious God-seeking. Prayer without ceasing is the "soul's sincere desire." Conscious and deliberate prayer is that sincere desire coming up into the intellect and taking shape there. It is unceasing prayer alone which makes occasional prayer easy and effectual.

§ 35. *For What? Topics of Prayer.* (See § 23.)

Mr. R. W. Emerson in his Essay on Self-Reliance (Essays, First Series, p. 67) says:—

"That which we call a holy office is not so much as brave or manly Prayer looks abroad, and asks for some foreign addition to come through some foreign virtue, and loses itself in endless mazes of natural and supernatural, and mediatorial and miraculous. Prayer that craves a particular commodity — any thing less than all good — is vicious. Prayer is the contemplation of the facts of life from the highest point of view. It is the soliloquy of a beholding and jubilant soul. It is the spirit of God pronouncing his works good. But prayer as a means to obtain a private end is meanness and theft. As soon as the man is at one with God, he will not beg. He will then see prayer in all action. The prayer of the farmer kneeling in his field to weed it, the prayer of the rower kneeling with the stroke of his oar, are true prayers heard through all nature, though for cheap ends."

Mr. Emerson here speaks in his Stoical mood. This view, so concisely expressed in the above passage, is the one we have been opposing through our whole Essay. Prayer *does* "look abroad and asks for some foreign addition," — for the man who prays has learned that his strength lies in passing out of his own small life, and opening himself to influences wholly above and beyond him. He has ceased to be self-sustained, and so is all-sustained. Prayer is *not* "contemplation," but, as Mr. Emerson, turning round at the end of the paragraph, himself says, it is action. It is *not* "soliloquy," but dialogue. To say, with Mr. Emerson at one moment, that prayer is contemplation, and then to call it action, — to say it is the soliloquy of the soul, and then to call it the utterance of the Spirit of God, — is to confound things which ought to be distinguished, — it is to "huddle and lump" what should be "sundered and divisible." Meditation is one thing, action is another. If we propose to reflect and meditate, let us say so, — let us not call it prayer.

Mr. Emerson objects to prayer which craves "a particular commodity," and then says that the farmer kneeling to weed his field makes a true prayer. But that is for a particular commodity, — for a cheap end. Is it prayer then, or is it not?

Undoubtedly Mr. Emerson *means* that we ought to work for these "commodities," and not to pray for them. But why then confound the two? Why call work by another name, not its own. Mr. Emerson defines prayer to be a soliloquy, a contemplation. Is there no distinction, then, between contemplation and action?

And can any one tell why it is brave and manly to work for a particular commodity, and vicious to pray for it. When my child is sick, I apply baths and use means to restore his health, — and I also ask God to bless those means. Why is the first "brave," and the second "meanness and theft"?

Was it meanness and theft in those who asked Jesus to come and heal their children, and did he encourage their meanness in going to them and helping them? If we may ask man's help in our difficulties, why may we not ask God's help, without this reproach? Is there a logician who can tell us that?

He who takes a Stoical view of God, nature, and man, will very naturally think it vicious to pray for any particular commodity. This view shuts God out of nature, and shuts man up in himself. It pushes independence and individuality in every thing to unlimited results. It sees only law, not love, in the relation of God to nature, and erects an order in the universe, salutary for classes, but cold to the individual. Providence is a benevolent Fate, and God's relation to the world is only that of Law-sustainer.

But with the view of God and of nature which we have endeavored to enforce as the Christian view, all objections to particular prayers fall away. We may ask for spiritual and for temporal blessings, — for Pardon, Peace, Truth, Strength, Joy, Love, — for opportunities of usefulness, — for wisdom to meet difficulties and conquer temptations. We may ask for ourselves and others, health, and all outward support, opportunity, and means. So too may we ask success in all our daily enterprises and labors.

We may ask for others, as for ourselves. There are those whom we can help in no other way, whom we can meet in no other way, whom we can meet and help in prayer. The mother's prayer for her absent child reaches far over the ocean, and on distant seas puts peace into his heart, and wisdom for imminent exigency into his mind.

We may pray for the living, and why not also for the dead? I believe that only Protestant hostility to the doctrine of Purgatory has caused the discontinuance of prayers for the dead. The doctrinal objection that the condition of the dead is finally determined, and cannot be altered by our prayers, has no foundation either in Scripture or Reason. That it has none appears from the proofs adduced in support of it, consisting usually of a text in Ecclesiastes, "In the place where the tree falleth, there it shall lie," and two lines of Dr. Watts, —

"There are no acts of pardon passed
In the cold grave to which we haste."

But there is absolutely nothing in the New Testament forbidding such prayers, and since they are prompted by natural feeling, this is equivalent to their permission, — on the principle, "If it were not so, I would have told you." Reason and the nature of things prompt us to believe that those who leave this world imperfect in character, enter the next state beyond this imperfect. They do not become so different from us, but that they may profit by our prayers still.

There is nothing, therefore, which interests us in this world, but may come specially before God in prayer. Things which man despises has God chosen. To him nothing is common or unclean, nothing insignificant which moves the hearts of his children. If trifles affect us, then let trifles be spoken of in our prayer, and that which is trifling in the topic will be lost in the interest of communion with our Heavenly Father.

§ 36. *To whom? Object of Prayer.*

An important question, not to be wholly passed over, concerns the Object of Prayer. To whom shall we pray?

1. The Unitarian answers, To the **Father** only.

2. The Trinitarian says, To the Father, the Son, the Holy Spirit, and the Trinity.

3. The Roman Catholic adds, Also the Virgin Mary and the Saints, — making a distinction, however, between *Latria* and *Dulia*, i. e. the sort of worship addressed to God and that to the saints.

The Unitarian in support of his position quotes the most positive texts of Scripture; for example, —

JOHN iv. 23. "The hour cometh and now is when the true worshippers shall worship THE FATHER in spirit and in truth," &c.

JOHN xvi. 23. "In that day" (namely, after Christ's resurrection) "ye shall *ask me nothing.* Verily, verily, I say unto you, Whatsoever ye shall *ask the Father* in my name, he will give it you."

LUKE xi. 2. "When ye pray, say, *Our Father.*"

The Unitarian also argues, that such a complex object of worship as is presented by the Trinity is adapted to confuse the mind, and that such a worship is in many respects exposed to the evils of polytheism.

But, on the other hand, the Trinitarian contends that God, out of Christ, is an abstraction, — incapable of meeting the wants of the heart. He says that God assumes a personal character as manifest in the flesh, and that we can speak to Him as to one near us, and having sympathy with us. The Trinitarian also endeavors to find support in the New Testament, contending that "to call on the Lord" is equivalent to prayer to Jesus.

The Roman Catholic defends the invocation of the saints by means of the distinction before referred to. He says that he does not worship the saints as he worships God, but differently. He addresses them as living beings, in a higher world, full of sympathy for those below, and asks *their* prayers and intercessions with God. If to ask a good man, who is yet in this world, to pray for you, involves nothing objectionable, and is not worship, why is it objectionable to ask him to pray for you, after he has gone into the other world? If we may pray for the dead, why may not the dead pray for us? If it be said that to ask any thing of an *invisible* being is to worship him, it may be replied that the question of worship cannot depend on the fact of visibility; otherwise it would be considered objectionable to ask any favor of a friend in the night-time, and a blind man ought to ask no favors at all. Or it may be said, that to ask of those in the other world implies their presence with worshippers in different lands, therefore their omnipresence, and therefore is giving to them a divine and incommunicable attribute of the Deity. But to this also the reply is easy. To be present in ten different places, or in a thousand different places, is not omnipresence. A man speaking in public is present by his thought to a thousand auditors at once, through the medium of sight and sound. A man who writes a book, or an article in the newspaper, is present by his thought to ten thousand readers in different places, through the medium of his book. The operator with an electric telegraph is present, through the medium of his wire, to all the offices on the route at the same moment. Therefore it may easily be that spirits out of the body may be present by their thought and perception, and by some medium of which we are now ignorant, to a great many persons and places at once. There is no impossibility, nor even any improbability, of this being the case. And, surely, if the

> "Saints on earth, and all the dead,
> But one communion make,"

this view will make the communion a reality, and will bring the other world much nearer to this one.

A practical objection, however, to this Roman

Catholic doctrine remains, and is not so easily disposed of. Granting the distinction between *Latria* and *Dulia*, between the worship paid to God and to the saints, will that distinction be regarded? Will it not be lost sight of in practice, and will not the saints, as being nearer to us, gradually attract to themselves all the worship, so that none remains to be paid to the Father? Facts authorize and confirm this fear. There is no doubt that, in Italy, nine tenths at least of all prayer is addressed to the Virgin, and goes no farther. Every city has its patron saint, who is the object of especial worship, and whose altar is thronged with kneeling devotees. Such is the case with Saint Januarius at Naples, Saint Charles Borromeo at Milan, and Saint Petronio at Bologna. A little incident occurred to us in the neighborhood of the latter city, which tends to show that the distinction of worship is often lost sight of. A party of travellers were descending the long portico leading to the Church of the Madonna of St. Luke, on the top of the Monte della Guardia, near Bologna, and met some children going up. We stopped to talk with them, and found they were going up to say their prayers to the saints and to the Madonna. We asked them in the course of the conversation which they loved best,

God or the saints. A bright boy about thirteen years old replied, — "We love them in the same way," — *nella stessa maniera.* If they loved them in the same way, they would be likely to worship them in the same way too. This shows that such invocation of saints is to be guarded with great care, and is attended with special dangers.

The result of this examination would therefore bring us to something like the following results.

1. All prayer should be addressed to the Father, but to the Father as revealed and manifested in the Son. We pray not to an abstract or philosophic God, but to Him who has shown himself to us in the life and teachings of Jesus, as a personal friend. We worship and adore Him who has shown himself in Christ so loving the world and so loving sinners as to wish to pardon all, and save every human being from the power and the guilt of sin. God, thus seen in Christ, is the only object of religious supplication and divine worship. He is the only ultimate source of all spiritual and temporal good.

2. Since we believe that Christ is with us always (Matt. xxviii. 20), that he has not left nor deserted the world, but is still near to it as a Saviour and Friend, we may speak to him as though

he were present, asking his sympathy, uttering our love, thanking him for his friendship. This has, in fact, been usual with Unitarians in their hymns, for all our hymn-books contain addresses to Jesus; as, for example, —

"Lord Jesus, come! for here
Our paths through wilds are laid," &c.

"Jesus, my living Head,
I bless thy faithful care," &c.

"Jesus, Prince of Peace, be near us,
Fix in all our hearts thy home."

3. The distinction between prayer to God and addresses to Christ consists in this, that we regard all that Christ has done or does for us as done by mediation, by intercession, by derived power. He is a dependent being, like ourselves, though so much higher and more exalted. Therefore, all that he has done for us we refer back to his Father and our Father, to his God and our God, as its ultimate source. And whatever we ask of him is in the way of mediation and intercession only.

4. But as there is danger of this distinction being forgotten in practice, it is best that all prayer, public or private, should be addressed to the Father through the Son, and that the Son him-

self be not addressed in supplication. There will still remain room for private and personal communion with Jesus, in the way of conversation rather than worship, — by hymns, by spontaneous expressions of love and trust and earnest interest, such as come naturally to the lips when we feel that an object of sincere attachment is near us, though unseen.

5. And the same is true as regards other departed spirits, whether those who are called saints, or any others. They are ministering spirits, they are objects of interest and affection. We are not *sure* that they are near us, or that they can hear us ; but, on the other hand, we are not sure of the contrary. So that if our heart prompts it, we may address them, we may open our soul to them, but not pray to them. Let prayer remain for God, whom we do know to be always near, and always conscious of our thoughts.

CHAPTER VI.

MOTIVES AND RESULTS.

§ 37. *Necessity and Advantage.*

To live without prayer is to live without communion with God. But this is to live away from God, and to separate ourselves from him as far as is possible for the human being to escape from his Maker. We cannot go away from the *power* of God, for that is around us at all times, and everywhere. We are leaning on his arm, upheld by his hand, consciously or unconsciously, at every moment. We cannot go away from the *love* of God. For that pursues, and surrounds, and blesses us still, however little we may deserve it. But we may go away from God by *turning away* from him, by forgetting him and neglecting him. We have the power of thus turning away, of closing our eyes inwardly, and opening them only outwardly; closing them toward heaven, and opening them toward earth.

We have this terrible freedom of escaping, if we choose, from the restraining sense of the Divine Presence, and so doing our own will, without the immediate rebuke of conscience. Most men are thus turned away, and it is this which makes it hard to pray and easy to sin. No man can pray earnestly and sin readily at the same time. We must either leave off sinning, or leave off praying. Consequently most men, whether they are great sinners or outwardly decent and moral, are really alienated from God. The proof of it is easy. It is, that, though He is always near to them, they are not aware of it, and the thought and sense of his nearness never restrains them from committing evil. The presence of a good man will restrain the tongue of the ribald and the profane, — the presence of the most insignificant human being influences them more or less, — but the presence of the Deity does not influence them at all. Therefore it is evident that they do not feel His presence, — that they are alienated from Him. Now, when we have repented of our sins, and determined to lead a religious life, and have begun to do so, we shall nevertheless find that this alienation from God has not become impossible. On the other hand, we shall find, in all probability, that, by allowing ourselves to commit apparently slight transgressions, we have again lost the quick sense of the surrounding God, and wandered again from our Father's house. In this case prayer becomes a matter of necessity, and prayer not as a gush of feeling, not as an indulgence of sentiment, but prayer as an act, an earnest act of turning to God, and holding the soul open to his influences, and to be fed and renewed by his inflowing life. The Christian comes to learn, by frequent experience, that he cannot live without prayer. And so he prays daily and hourly, not as a duty, but as a necessity, — prays *when* it is necessary, be it seldom or often, — prays *till* the need is supplied, till the hunger has ceased, till the empty soul is filled, till his weakness has been made strength, till his weariness has changed to inward rest. And then, having prayed from necessity, he prays again spontaneously, the prayer of thanksgiving and gratitude, the acknowledgment of this new life. And if again he finds himself astray, he prays by confessing his sin, by owning his estrangement, by beseeching pardon and reconciliation and peace. And when in union with God, and not praying from necessity, or for himself, he prays for others; he prays for the kingdom of God, for the coming of peace, truth, and love to the world;

he prays for union in the Church, for practical Christianity among Christians, for the ignorant, the poor, the afflicted, for the slave and the oppressed, for the vicious and abandoned, for the infidel and the heathen. Then also he finds pleasure in remembering before God individuals. He intercedes for his friends, according to what he supposes their needs, temptations, and trials may be. He enjoys bringing them, one by one, before the mercy-seat, and doing for them in prayer what he can do for them in no other way. Thus we pray, from such motives as these. Out of *necessity*, because we are away from God, and are therefore weak, and *must* pray to gain strength; because we are wretched, and must pray in order to gain comfort. Out of *gratitude*, because our heart is happy, our cup full, our life advancing; and joy overflows into prayer. Out of *love*, because we wish to help our brother, our sister, and we cannot help them in any other way than this. Out of interest in Christ's cause, out of wish to make his kingdom, out of faith in the good time near at hand. Out of *penitence*, because we cannot find peace till we go to our Father and say, "God be merciful to me a sinner!"

§ 38. *Prayer a Duty or a Privilege.*

Next let us look more closely at the relation of prayer to our other duties.

In using the phrase "other duties," I have implied that prayer *is* a duty; and in one sense it may be so considered. It is a duty to pray, just as it is a duty to live on terms of affectionate intimacy and intercourse with our father and our mother, our wife and children. But it is not a duty in the sense in which it is our duty to tell the truth or to pay our debts. In other words, it does not belong to that class of duties in which the outward act is the principal thing. A man ought to tell the truth, he ought to pay his debts, no matter in what frame of mind he does it. But what would you think of a son or daughter who should make it a rule to go to their father so many times a day, and express their gratitude to him in a formal manner for his love and paternal care exercised over them? The moment that the expression of affection was made a duty, in this sense of the word, the moment it became a formality, a task-work, a piece of routine, you would expect it to become a cold and difficult matter enough, and you would not wonder to hear the child complaining that his filial affections were growing very cold, under such a system. But in the same way we often freeze our religious affections, by making it a mere matter of duty to pray so much and so often every day, instead of regarding prayer in its truer light as the highest joy, the freest and happiest privilege allotted to us here below.

The whole life of a religious man falls into two grand divisions, and all his actions belong to the one or the other. The one is the region of *piety*, the other the region of *morality*. Piety and morality, united, make up *religion*, or the whole life of a Christian. The region of morality is under the Law; it is a stern and rugged clime, a land of restraint, of effort, of struggle, of battle. The performance of duty, the doing the work of the Lord, this is the problem of morality. Here the Christian must be ready to labor, to endure constraint, to undergo hardship, to fight the good fight of faith, to do with his might whatever his hand finds to do, knowing that there is neither work, nor device, nor knowledge, nor wisdom, in the grave, whither he is hastening.

But when our overtasked strength faints amid the toils of life, when we are weary and heavy laden, then we turn into that other land, — the land of the Gospel, of pious trust and joy, —

where the heart can repose in the bosom of God, and abide under the shadow of the Almighty. This should not be a land of constraint, but of freedom. Joy and love, faith and hope, a happy sense of a divine guardianship, — these are the angel spirits which hover over that divine region. There is no fear in love, for perfect love casteth out fear. Where the spirit of the Lord is, there is liberty.

But now it is a sad mistake when that part of our life which should be free and light as air is bound with chains, — when that which should be a joy becomes a task, — when the staff which should sustain us is added to the burden which oppresses us, — when the cordial of refreshment is changed into the bitter cup of trial. Yet this is done when we make moral duties out of Christian privileges. Prayer, if any thing, should be the most solemnly joyful act of our lives. How often it is degraded into a task! The Sabbath, if any thing, should be a day of rest and refreshment for the weary body and the weary soul. How often it is transformed into the heaviest burden we have to carry! The Church, the assembling together of Christian friends, should be the happiest meeting in the world; *there* should be seriousness without gloom, earnestness without anxiety, cheerfulness without excess, freedom yet order, a pervading sympathy of heart, felt rather than spoken. Instead of this, what do we often have? Frozen forms, of which time has eaten away the once living core; a heavy, languid, indolent multitude going through a dreary routine from a sense of duty, — listening to scholastic harangues, or rhetorical orations, or theological quibbles.

What is the cause of all this? It comes from disregarding the limits of things, confounding together the different parts of life, not distinguishing what ought to be distinguished, and so losing piety in morality.

Piety and morality ought not to be, and cannot be, separated in any man's life; but they can be distinguished, though not separated. Piety cannot exist without morality, nor morality without piety, yet they are not the same thing. So the stalk cannot exist without the root, nor the root without the stalk; yet they are not the same thing, nor should their spheres be confounded. It would not do to put the stalk into the ground and the root in the air. Nor is it right or wise to subject prayer, which is a part of piety, to those constraints which properly belong to morality.

There is one class of Christians who make

piety the whole of religion; there is another class who make morality the whole of religion. I believe that there is a third and increasing class, who have learned that religion is made up of *both*, — that these are the two faces, the opposite poles, of the religious life, — and who know how to distinguish them without dividing them.

In describing the true way to cultivate the spirit of prayer, we must say that to pray *merely* as a duty rather hinders than helps it. But let the mind and heart be pervaded with the conviction of those great truths which constitute the Gospel, — the character of God as our spiritual Friend and Father; the mission of Christ as the Saviour of the soul from sin and ruin; the promise of the Holy Spirit to all believers who seek for it; the love, the trust, the encouragement, the promises of the Gospel, the everlasting presence of a spiritual Friend; God nigh at hand and in our heart, as the Comforter, the Holy Spirit. Sinking deep into the centre of these truths, and so being filled with a spirit of trust, never to be shaken, in God as our tenderest friend, we shall always be ready to come boldly to the throne of grace to find help in time of need. We shall have that sense of a Divine Presence which shall cause us to pray without ceasing, — though our prayers will be often only a throb of gratitude, or a sudden aspiration of love, or the soul falling down in humility, and bowing itself before God. And then, too, we shall find a place and a use for times of prayer, and for a certain degree of method and system in prayer. For we have already seen and said that spiritual and true prayer need not be immethodical and without system. On the contrary, every one can see that some method is right here, and necessary, as in other things. It does not prove my friendship insincere, that I say to my friend when we part, "Let us write to each other at least twice a week," or, "Let us look every evening, at a certain hour, at a particular star, and think of one another." If the letter-writing and star-looking are done *merely* as a duty, it will be bad, and if the method of prayer be retained when its life is gone, this is also bad. But every pious heart must feel that God, in the very arrangements of nature, and in the ordinances of the heavens, says to us, "In the morning think of me, in that calm hour which I send you before the toil and din of life commences; and in the evening think of me; after it is over, when the holy stars pour quiet upon the earth, then remember me." And so, too, on the Sabbath day, we shall rejoice in the opportunity for a closer walk with God. Times and forms have their place, and their use. But do not let the soul wear them, as David wore the cumbrous armor of Saul, which he had not proved, and which was only an encumbrance.

The whole of the teaching and example of Jesus on the subject of prayer confirms the view we have now taken. He does not speak of prayer as a duty, but as a privilege. He does not lay down strict and formal rules for prayer; he does not *command* fixed hours of prayer. He tells us *not* to use vain repetitions, not to think to be heard for our much speaking. It is, "Ask, and ye shall receive." This is the motive for prayer which he sets before us. And in the parable which teaches, "that men *ought* always to pray, and not to faint," we see that this "*ought*" means only to encourage us to persevere in prayer, and not be discouraged because the strength or the peace which we need does not immediately come. And the fact that every thing which is told us of the prayers of Jesus is so *incidental*, proves that he himself gave no countenance to the prayer of mere duty.

There are those, doubtless, who may apprehend danger from such a view as this. They will fear that, except men be urged to pray as a duty, they will not pray even as much as they do now. And undoubtedly this is true to a certain extent. Those who have been praying merely from a sense of duty will be glad to leave off praying altogether, and with them to "pray without ceasing" will amount to not praying at all. It is unquestionably the case, that, when prayer is enjoined as a duty, there is a great deal more of the *form* of prayer than when it is made the free-will offering of the heart. Nowhere in Christendom is there so much earnest *outward* prayer as in Mohammedan countries. There, when the hour of prayer is sounded from the minaret, men fall on their knees in the streets, in the market, wholly absorbed in the act, so that you might almost run over them and they would not notice you. Nowhere in Protestant churches is there such absorbed and constant prayer as among the Catholics. "At that time," says Luther in his Table-talk, "my wife asked me, 'How is it that in the Romish Church there is so much and such fervent prayer, while we are very cold and careless in our praying?'". The answer of the Reformer, though ungraciously worded, had a truth in it, — "The Devil," says he, "drives them to pray." It is the spirit of constraint, of anxiety, of fear; not of love, or cheerful faith, which makes up a great deal of such prayer. And so, in Protestant communions, those who take the most liberal views will always be found behind the others in religious zeal and the observances of piety. But what then? We do not find that all this formal prayer tends to build up a holier or more godly life in Mohammedan countries than in Christian; in Catholic countries than in Protestant; in the stricter sects of Protestantism than in the more free. I do not find that Episcopacy, with its forms, has made a more godly people than Quakerism, with its extreme and utter informality. Yet let us not run into either extreme. Let us *use* forms, and observe seasons and times, so that they may help us, and not hinder us.

§ 39. *The Holy Spirit.*

The great result of Prayer is the gift of the Holy Spirit. This was given originally in the Christian Church in answer to prayer, either of the believer himself, or of some one else for him. The order of the Christian life was, first, Faith; next, Repentance; next, the Holy Spirit. The gift of the Holy Spirit was in order to make the believer wholly a Christian, and no one was considered to be a Christian wholly till he had received the Holy Ghost. By Faith he became a Christian in thought, by Repentance he became a Christian in action, and then by the Holy Spirit he was made a Christian in heart and life. But all which he himself needed to do, in order to receive this gift, was to believe in it, and to ask for it. Without it, he stood on the lower plane of a mere believer in Christianity; with it, he had Christ formed within him, the hope of glory. He was made thus a living Christian, full of faith, hope, and love. From this fulness of inward life, his outward life came, as the stream flows from its fountain, pushed forward for ever by a power behind. It was this inward life, hidden with Christ in God, which gave him energy, gave him patience, gave him insight and foresight, fitted him for his sphere and work, made him ready to live or to die.

The gift of the Holy Spirit, then, at first, was an essential part of the Christian's life. Is it any less essential now? Can we be truly and livingly and effectually Christians, without constant prayer to God for his Spirit, and the constant reception of it as daily bread, the source of daily life? I see not how. I see a poor and meagre Christianity, built up by opinions about Jesus, exerting itself to fulfil a sphere of duty more or less extended; — but how cold and cheap a thing is this compared with Christian life! What we need is a life steadily fed from within by God, a life of Insight, of Foresight, of Love, of Action. This life should develop at once every individual tendency in the soul, and also those deeper convictions and aims in which all souls are one. But let us see further what this life is, and what are its results.

§ 40. *Christ in the Heart. — Inward Life.*

The Life which results from Prayer is, in the first place, the life of Christ in the heart. This alone makes one fully a Christian. For, according to the New Testament, Christianity is not a creed, nor a transient emotion, nor an outward behavior, but an inward and an outward life. It is called in the New Testament by this name, but with the adjective "Eternal," in order to distinguish it from temporal or bodily life. For Eternal Life, in the New Testament, by no means implies immortality, or a continuation of our outward existence, but much rather inward immortality, or spiritual life. As temporal life is the life of the soul in time, fed out of time, so eternal life is that life of the soul which is fed out of eternity. It is not merely continued existence;

for while, as we believe, all will continue to exist, eternal life is conditional; it comes through faith, — through faith in Jesus and his words, — "the meat which endureth unto everlasting life." (John vi. 27.) It is continually repeated, that "whosoever *believeth in Jesus* shall have everlasting life." (John iii. 15, 16.) It is also said, that eternal life already commences in this world, and that "he that believeth hath everlasting life *abiding in him*"; which also indicates a present, and not a future immortality. And yet again we read, that "this is life eternal, to *know*" God and Christ; which implies that it is a state of conviction, an inward life.

The natural type and emblem of this higher life is our bodily life. As the body lives by means of the indwelling soul, so the soul lives by means of the indwelling spirit. The soul of man which gives life to the body receives itself a higher life from the spirit. By means of the soul, the body ceases to be a machine, only moved by external forces, but is filled and pervaded throughout with an activity of its own. And so by means of the spirit the soul ceases to be moved and swayed by the world without, by earthly passions and desires, but reacts freely from its own steadfast convictions and purposes, moves freely toward its own chosen aim. This steadfast life is that which Christ promised his disciples as the gift of the Holy Spirit. He continually dwells upon it in the last chapters of John, as that which is to make all things new within their souls, to give them new convictions of truth, to bring all things to their remembrance, and to teach them more hereafter than they were then capable of receiving. The Holy Spirit was to be the Comforter, to comfort them in the outward absence of their Master, by bringing them inwardly near to him. He continually repeats, in every varying way, that the Holy Spirit is a divine influence on the heart to bring them near to himself. "He shall take of mine, and shall show it unto you." "He shall testify of me." So that it is in fact Christ himself returning inwardly to them, after having left them outwardly. This Comforter, the Spirit of Truth, who was to abide with them for ever, whom the world did not know but whom they knew, who dwelt with them and was to be in them, — what was this but Christ himself? This he says in express terms: "I will not leave you comfortless, I will come to you." He predicts the most intimate union between his disciples, himself, and God, — whoever loves him shall see him, shall live by his life. (John xiv. 15–23.) And this is not to be a transient visit, but a permanent abode. "My Father and I will love him, and we will come to him, and *make our abode* with him."

Now, who does not see that this inward, personal communion with Christ, through the medium of the Father's influence, is the one thing most needed, both for private and public Christianity. Because we are not living thus inwardly near to Christ, inwardly fed by his life, our souls want strength, beauty, peace, profound conviction, and power. We are weak and vacillating, because we have only opinions and not convictions. Instead of knowing God and knowing Christ, instead of seeing the truth, we have only probable belief concerning it. Instead of a fixed aim steadily pursued, we are swayed to and fro by the fluctuations of worldly opinions around us. Instead of inward peace and satisfaction, derived from constant intercourse with God and constant reception of his forgiving love, we are beset with discontent, self-reproach, and spiritual anxiety. Thus weak in ourselves, we cannot make others strong. Having nothing ourselves, we can give nothing to others; for it is giving *ourselves* which does good.

> "Not what we give, but what we share,
> For the gift without the giver is bare."

Therefore we cannot be what every Christian ought to be, — the "salt of the earth," the "light of the world," a fixed axis around which other things shall revolve. The Christian who is inwardly near to Christ, is like one who should be able to see the stars in the daytime, and thus have the power to determine the position and direction of every thing around him. He ought to give law to the world; to judge it, its maxims, its customs, by a higher standard, — to be always its censor, its sibyl, its oracle. But without the inward life he is able to do nothing of this, he becomes a mere echo of the public opinion about him, and he loses all power of real usefulness.

Perhaps it may be said, that, as long as the Christian has the Bible in his hands, he ought to be able to resist this tendency. But we read the Bible as we read every thing else, by means of our own experience, and by the light of our own present belief. We see in it more or less what we bring with us. The truths in the Bible must be spiritually discerned. Every thing that we read we necessarily translate as we read it, so as to bring it into some harmony with our previous stock of ideas Hence the Bible is made to teach all sorts of doctrines, to defend all kinds of abuses, to oppose every reform, and keep the world and Church from the development which God intends. The Bible is made an anchor holding the Church fast in the flowing current of time, instead of a compass by which its course may be guided to more blessed shores. Therefore, to understand the Bible, we need an inward life, rooted in Christ, and fed by the Holy Spirit.

Now, there are three false views of the Holy Spirit, which, at the present day, prevent our Christianity from being a life; prevent us from realizing this constant peace which is also light and strength; prevent us from being able to say that "our life is hid with Christ in God," and from understanding the Apostle when he declares, "I live, yet not I, but Christ who lives in me." These false views of the Holy Spirit are those which make its influences arbitrary, — which make its influences irresistible, — and which make of it a third person distinct from Christ himself. Taking either of these views, we are impeded in our prayers, or prevented from praying the prayer of Faith.

An opinion prevails in the Church, that the Holy Spirit is given arbitrarily, and not according to any fixed law. Men speak of the Holy Spirit as coming and going, as sometimes being in one place and sometimes in another; they speak of God's withholding it, and often show in their prayers that they are quite uncertain as to whether the Spirit will be given or not. Of course they cannot pray the prayer of Faith, but only a doubtful and hesitating prayer. The Holy Spirit ceases to be an habitual presence, God and Christ making their abode in the heart, but becomes a transient influence, a sudden incursion of God into the soul; it is no longer the still, small voice, but rather the whirlwind and the fire. But this view is surely opposed to the whole doctrine and spirit of the New Testament. Christ teaches that the Holy Spirit is *always* given to those who ask it, and that it would be as impossible for God to refuse it, as for a good parent to give his child a stone instead of a piece of bread. And accordingly, throughout the New Testament, it is assumed that these divine influences make up a constant part of the Christian life. Christians are taught to pray "in the Holy Spirit"; the Spirit is said "to dwell in us"; we are taught that we are "led" by it, that it gives us our faith in Christ, gives us the sense that we are the children of God, enables us to call God Father, helps us to pray, and is, in sum, the source of every part of a Christian's life. All Christians drink into one spirit, and though they have various gifts of faith or knowledge, yet the source of all is the same. We are to "live in the Spirit," and "walk in the Spirit," and "sow to the Spirit," and so we shall have "the fruit of the Spirit, love, joy, and peace." Its influences are compared with the regular operations of nature. If we sow to the Spirit, we shall of the Spirit reap life everlasting. It is a steady light and warmth in the soul, which we are not to quench; a friend ever near, whom we are not to grieve away. Therefore we may be sure that at every moment, under all circumstances, God is waiting to be gracious; we have only to open the door of the heart, and he enters; we have only to turn in to the depths of the soul, and we find our life, "our life hid with Christ in God."

Another false view concerning the Holy Spirit is that which makes of it a separate person from Christ himself. The Scripture view, as given in the Gospel of John, is, as we have seen, that through God's influence on the heart we are brought into inward relation with Christ. For as Christ brings us to the Father, so the Father leads us to the Son. Thus God and Christ come and make their abode in the heart. He who believes this always prays to God to be brought near to Christ; the object to whom he prays is the Father, the aim of his prayer is union with the Father and the Son. But now, if, instead of this simple and exquisite relation, instead of this union with the Father and the Son for which Christ prayed, asking it for his disciples, we have a third and distinct personality introduced, it not only confuses the mind, but interferes with the great object of the prayer. We know what we need when we ask for Christ, for we have his historic life and his recorded words as a guide. We know what Christian experience is, we know Faith, Hope, Love, Humility, Patience; but the Holy Spirit, *as a separate person*, we do not know. Consequently there is something foreign in this idea. It does not mingle easily with the regular flow of the Christian life. It is always looked for as a preternatural influence out of the course of nature; and, consequently, with this view of the Holy Spirit, our prayers will be less regular, less constant, less connected with the fulness of Christian life. Hence it is that those who, in theory, accept the doctrine of the distinct personality of the Holy Spirit, set it aside so much in their prayers. The devotions of Christendom do not recognize the Holy Spirit as the object of prayer, in the same way that they recognize the Father and the Son. Most of the devotion of the Church is offered to the Father, as Christ directed all to be. But for consistency's sake, and also because there is a personal attachment to Jesus, a small portion, perhaps a fifth or a tenth part of the whole, is addressed to him. But seldom indeed is the Holy Spirit addressed as a distinct person. So much wiser are Christian instincts than Christian opinions. Yet these false opinions come in to confuse and trouble the mind, and, so far as they exercise any influence, exercise a pernicious one.

The third false view to which I referred is that which makes the influence of the Spirit irresistible. This view, directly opposed to the Scripture, comes only from the desire for logical consistency in those who accept a Calvinistic view of divine influence. The Scripture tells us not to "quench the Spirit," not to "grieve the Spirit," to "draw nigh to God and he will draw nigh to us." The doctrine of the Scripture is, that it is always in our power to open or to close the door of the heart; that it becomes closed to God by sin; that all wilfulness, worldliness, anxiety, selfishness, shuts out God and Christ. Then the soul is left barren, cold, empty, incapable of any true virtue. What can we do then? We cannot by an act of the will create within the heart Christian sentiments and graces; we cannot by moral effort create within the soul generosity or love. What *can* we do? We can open the door; we can let God's influence come into the heart to lead us to Christ, to give us a sense of his pardoning love, to lift us to a higher plane of conviction. And this is *prayer* in its most essential nature.

When we take this view of prayer, — when the Church takes this view, — what a change will take place in the inward life of Christians! Those views of Christianity which are now thought mystical, will be seen to be the only truly rational ones. The doctrines of Christian perfection which are regarded as heresies, being better understood, will be recognized as integral parts of Christian truth. It will be seen that the whole of a Christian's life must flow from God and Christ, and that prayer, or keeping open the soul to God, must be without ceasing. It will be seen that to live in the Spirit is the only true life; that we are away from ourselves when we are away from God; that to keep ourselves thus in the love of God is in reality easier than to alternate from moods of worldliness to moods of piety. Then the word Piety will no more indicate something strange or foreign, something grafted into the soul from without, but will be seen to be the life of the soul according to its own highest law. This piety will be in nothing ascetic; it will be full of joy and cheerfulness, because it partakes every day of the true wine of life. It will have no anxiety about outward things, or inward things, trusting always in God for all. It will not seek as its aim to save its soul, knowing that its soul is safe while it is near God. It will not serve God from hope of heaven, or fear of hell, but because his service is perfect freedom. Its goodness will not be that of effort and struggle, its life will not be hard work, but God working within the heart to will and to do of his good pleasure. Its maxim will not be, "To work is to pray," but "Work *out of* Prayer." And its prayer will be thanksgiving and gratitude, together with supplication, for perfect love will have cast out fear.

"Heavenly Father, Life Divine!
Change my nature into thine!
Move and spread throughout my soul,
Actuate and fill the whole!
Be it I no longer now
Living in the flesh, but Thou."

§ 41. *Christ in the Character. — Moral Culture.*

The effect of Prayer when thus explained as Life flowing from God, is very important in its moral results. If our aim be the perfection of our moral nature, we may set about it in two ways. We may make direct attempts for the cultivation of certain virtues, and for the repression of certain vices, taking them up one by one as a matter of discipline. Or, we may labor on the whole instead of the parts, by living in the Spirit, living near to God and Christ, and so learning also to walk in the Spirit. Both methods are good, but the second is the most thorough. It is the method of Nature, which works upon all parts of the plant at the same time, by filling the whole with life. The great thing needed for moral development is more vital power. Love will make all things new. A profound influence in the centre of the soul will cause all parts of life to bud and blossom and bear fruit.

This great change in the character produced by a new inward life flowing from God, is continually referred to and described in the New Testament. It is "putting off the old man, and putting on the new man, who after God is created in righteousness and true holiness." It is spoken of as the "fruit of the Spirit, love, joy, peace, long-suffering, gentleness, goodness, faith, meekness, temperance." It is building one's self up in the Holy Ghost. It is described as becoming a new creature: "If any man be in Christ, he is a new creature; old things have passed away, all things have become new." And how these expressions are illustrated by the wonderful change which took place in the characters of the Apostles after the Ascension of Jesus, and the gift of the Holy Ghost! Certainly they all became new creatures; certainly old things passed away, and all things became new. What an immense development took place in each under the influence of this inward life flowing from God! How the specialities of character in Peter, James, John, Paul, were brought out by the indwelling spirit. It did not give an outward discipline, but an inward development. It was not training, but education, that is, the *educing* each man's most intimate and special character, as the sun of spring educes the life of every seed according to the separate law of its organization. This is the difference between moral training and moral education. Moral training gives us some outward type to be imitated, some outward example to be followed, some outward law to be obeyed. But moral education is the growth of the soul, "first the blade, then the ear, afterward the full corn in the ear." Now, religion has been made too much an outward discipline, and too little an inward development. Men have been trained according to some one type of character; in the Catholic Church by the rule of different orders, the rule of St. Benedict, the rule of St. Francis, or St. Loyola. And moral discipline as laid down in Protestant books of ethics has been always too much an outward conformity to some excellent model, too little a growth from within. But in the New Testament it is not so. We do not read there of the Imitation even of Christ, and nothing is said of modelling one's self after Christ, much less after Paul or John. What we are to do is not to imitate Christ, but to "grow up in all things into him who is our head, even Christ Jesus."

In this growth was shown the possibility of unfolding individual distinctions, even while obeying a common law. They grew up by the same Christian progress into identity and diversity, into the most profound central unity of conviction, aim, experience, — into the most marked diversity of taste, tendency, faculty. Peter, James, John, Paul, — how wholly different from each other do they appear in their writings, and yet how profoundly at one in their central convictions! The unity and variety of character in these four Apostles is the sufficient proof of what otherwise might seem doubtful, that a profound spiritual influence develops all that is individual in character, while it brings all these individualities into harmony with each other.

These varieties of development, unfolded under the influence of the Holy Spirit, seem to be described in the New Testament, by the phrase "gifts of the Spirit." The description given us by Paul (1 Cor. xii.) of spiritual gifts, points directly at this variety in harmony, which, as it has been called the principle of beauty, may also be called the principle of goodness. Paul speaks of diversities of gifts, but the same Spirit, and how the Spirit gives to one man the word of wisdom, to another the word of knowledge, and the like. He compares this variety in unity to the variety in unity of the human body. His purpose in this place leads him to regard this variety of Christian faculty as resulting from variety of spiritual influence; but though he does not give the reason for the variety, nor say why the Spirit should give to one man wisdom, and to another man knowledge, we cannot suppose that this is *without* rea son, or arbitrary. As no reason is given, we are at liberty to assume that reason which is the most probable, and accordingly we may infer that the influence of the Spirit developed various faculties, according to original differences of organization. In this case, the development being sudden made it seem more like a pure gift. A man finds himself suddenly in the possession of a special faculty, the power of prophecy, of healing, of working miracles, and he naturally regards it as a new faculty imparted by God wholly *ab extra.* But there was probably the basis in his nature for the special gift. The influence *ab extra* was the same Divine Spirit, but within each individual was to be found the reason of the diversity of result.

But the great difference between moral training and moral growth is to be found in the different motive power and the difference in the results. Moral training is a painful struggle from a sense of duty to form habits of virtue by the mere force of individual will. Moral growth is a happy unfolding of spiritual faculties from love to God, and by the power of his indwelling Spirit. In the one case it is all struggle and conflict, in the other it is life and growth. In the one case it is a task carried on with anxiety and discouragement; in the other no task, no toil, but the opening of the heart to receive heavenly gifts, in the firm faith that all needful power will be imparted. And because anxiety palsies and weakens, because confidence gives strength, therefore the success in the two methods is also very different. The great power in man which enables him to accomplish important results for himself or others, is not the unaided will, but the faculty of putting himself in harmony with the great tides of life which flow from God, and flow through the race. He who works from himself can do something, but he who works from God can do every thing. "I can do nothing of myself," is the still stronger statement of the Apostle, — "I can do all things through Christ who strengthens me."

When, therefore, prayer shall become the element of all Christian life, when the heart shall be always kept open toward God, when we shall live in the Spirit, and walk in the Spirit, and thus have God and Christ abiding within us, there will be a great development of moral character in all directions. The virtues now painfully cultivated, starveling plants pinched by frost and withered by heat, will grow up fair and fruitful out of this inward life. Christian character will not be formed after one model, nor a monotonous repetition of external forms, but healthfully varied by all that is original and free and natural in human organization. Then shall virtue be also beauty, not harsh and hard conscience, not crabbed morality, but graceful and harmonious as the sights and sounds of nature.

> "Serene shall be our day and bright,
> And happy shall our nature be,
> When love is an unerring light,
> And joy its own security."

§ 42. *Christ in the Church. — Christian Union and Coöperation.*

When prayer thus pervades all of life, its influence will be felt in the Church, in many new ways. The prayers of the Church are now more or less spasmodic and irregular. The ideas of the Church concerning the answer to prayer make of it too much a magical influence, disturbing the laws of the mind. When instead of this, the answer to prayer is seen to be a part of the universal order, and prayer thus becomes regulated, and is the source of all our activity, a love will flow from God into the Christian Church, which will enable it, first, to be in union with itself, and, secondly, to convert the world. The life of God flowing first into the individual soul, then developing all forms of Christian character, will afterward bring the Christian Church into its true unity.

The great need of the Protestant Church at the present time is union, as the great need of the Roman Catholic Church is freedom. This union is sought for by Protestants in all ways; they try to produce a unity of *form* like that of the Catholics, but they find it impossible; they try to produce unity of *opinion* by means of creeds, but every new creed is like a wedge introduced into a denomination to split it in twain. By and by it will be seen, that the union needed is not that of opinion, nor of form, but unity of spirit and action. The power of the Protestant Church is in its sects; its weakness is in its sectarianism. Its sects, with their various forms of opinion, worship, and religious manifestation, adapt themselves to all varieties of human character. Those who cannot be moved by the Episcopalians are converted by the Methodists; those who are not reached by the Presbyterians are found by the Quakers; a peculiar class of minds are fed out of the cup of Swedenborg; and some who cannot believe without their understanding, or against their reason, come naturally to the Unitarians.

Thus one sect is the hand, one the eye, one the foot, one the brain, and one the heart, — many members, but not one body. This variety of administration is the power and beauty of Protestantism. But the mutual hostility of its sects is its weakness and disgrace. The Church needs not that its sects should be abolished, but that their sectarian hostility should be destroyed; that they should no longer contend, but coöperate. They should come to a mutual understanding, and arrange a system of coöperation. In every city, in every village, there should be a central organization in which all sects should be represented, and which should determine the sphere of activity for each. To the Methodists should be assigned one part of the field of labor, to the Presbyterians another, to the Episcopalians a third. Where the Methodists could do the most good, their Church should be established, and all the other sects work therein; where some other denomination could do the most good, that should be established by a general agreement.

The difficulty which now makes such coöperation impossible is quite apparent. It is, that each sect considers itself, not as a sect, but as the whole. Episcopalians think that everybody should become Episcopalians; Methodists are persuaded that Methodism is to swallow up all the Church; Calvinists suppose that it is essential for every one to accept the creed of Calvin. Instead of considering themselves integral parts of the body, — a hand, a foot, an eye, which would be honor enough, — they consider themselves the whole body. While this notion prevails, there can of course be no such thing as union. Now what is to correct this narrowness? I see no hope but in a deeper Christian life. For it is evident that the union of Forms and the union of Opinion are neither practicable nor desirable. There is no probability that any one of the existing Protestant sects is to absorb into itself all the rest, nor that any one of the different creeds is to swallow all the others. The tendency still continues the other way. Every year, new sects and new creeds present themselves. Nor is such a result desirable, were it practicable; for no existing forms or creeds are the best absolutely, but each of them is the best relatively. One form, one creed, is the best for one class of minds, — another form, another creed, is the best for another class of minds.

It is impossible for the bigot or the sectarian to understand this, for to them their creed and sect is the equivalent of Christianity. The one is narrow-minded, the other is narrow-hearted, and the cure for the narrow mind and the narrow heart is equally to be found in a deeper Christian experience. This will lead the narrow-minded man into larger insight, and the narrow-hearted man into larger love. The man who has been accustomed to regard his creed as an adequate statement of Christian truth, finds, as he passes into a deeper religious life, that new views open continually before him. For life is the light of man. It is not knowledge which is the source of life, but life which is the source of knowledge. That is to say, all new knowledge comes to us from experience ; knowledge of outward things through sensible experience, knowledge of spiritual things through spiritual experience. Reflection, on the contrary, which clears up, arranges, and defines our knowledge, thereby limits it. The substance of truth comes to us through experience, the form of truth through reflection. Hence, while reflection, in the form of theology, defines, arranges, bounds, it necessarily limits ; fencing in the truth which we possess, it fences out that which we have not yet obtained. But Christian experience leads us on to fresh fields and pastures new ; enables us to find a soul of truth, where we have supposed that there was only unmixed error, and thus produces a true Christian liberality.

Hence we find that spiritual Christians are seldom bigots. The more deep and thorough their Christian experience, the more are they able to recognize elements of truth in the opinions of others; the higher they ascend toward God, the wider is the horizon of truth which they command. Their test of Christianity is the life of Christ in the soul, and they recognize this as being present amid a great variety of opinions. Where this divine life exists, they are sure that essential truth cannot be wanting, and this life is to them the one thing needful; where it is, they find a brother, they are drawn toward it by an irresistible attraction, and their deepest sympathies are with all who love the Lord Jesus Christ in sincerity. The affinities of the sectarian are with those who accept the same forms with himself, the affinities of the theologian are with those who accept the same opinions with himself; but the affinities of the spiritual man are with those who have the same inward life with himself. The sectarian does not care much what a man's opinions are, nor what his Christian experience is, provided he will join his Church, and accept his forms. The true Church being accepted, he thinks that every thing else will come. He is, therefore, often quite liberal as regards differences of opinion and states of heart; he will admit into his Church heretics, publicans, and sinners, but he is relentless toward those who prefer another denomination or form of worship to his. The bigot, on the other hand, does not care much what a man's denomination is, nor what his Christian experience is, provided he believes a certain creed; the true creed being accepted, he thinks that every thing else will come. He may, therefore, be liberal toward members of other sects, but is relentless toward those who differ from him on any point of theological opinion. Meantime, the man of deeper Christian experience feels sure that, where Christ is formed in the soul, all essential truth and all important external forms will come. The unity, therefore, which he desires, is the unity of the spirit in the bond of peace.

Therefore, when Jesus stood among his disciples collected for the last time, and prayed with them, he prayed for this union among Christians, flowing out of their union with God and with himself. He prayed that they might be all one, as he was one with God. Therefore it was not for an ecclesiastical, or doctrinal, but for a spiritual union, that he besought the Father in this solemn, supreme hour. And now the Christian Church, having tried in succession, and tried in vain, the experiment of ecclesiastical and formal union, will try, and try successfully, its last great experiment of a unity in the spirit flowing out of the life of Christ. This being established, the Church will be perfectly at one. Peace will be within its walls, and prosperity within its palaces. And so, inwardly united and at one with itself, it will be able to go forward with confidence toward the conversion of the world.

§ 43. *Christ in the World.*

When the prayer of faith, returning into the Church, has thus made the Church at one, it will then have power to manifest Christ to the world. Then the world will believe that God has sent him. For the heathen world cannot be converted to Christ till Christendom becomes truly Christian; Christian nations will not become really Christian till the Church is at one in the life of Christ, and the Church will only thus become at one as individual Christians learn to pray the prayer of faith, and to live in the spirit of that prayer. Christ enters first into the individual heart, next into the collective life of the Church, then into the life of Christian nations, and shall at last come to reign the true King of the world. Then every knee shall bow, and every tongue confess him to be Lord, to the glory of God the Father.

The slow progress of Christianity in the world has been a source of doubt and discouragement from the first. "Where is the promise of his coming?" was a question anxiously asked even in the days of the Apostles, and it is anxiously asked still. Everything seems to remain as it was, everything to go on as it did. The reign of Christ was to be a reign of peace, but war still rages among the nations. Christ was to break every yoke, but slavery still exists, and that even in our own land. The poor were to have the Gospel preached to them, but the practical Gospel of love is not so preached as yet. All were to be taught of God, and to know him, but ignorance prevails throughout Christendom. Unjust distinctions, excessive luxury, gross vices, still continue throughout the world. When, then, is Christ to come, and what shall be the signs of his coming? What shall be the signs of the end of the heathen age, and the beginning of the Christian era?

The progress of Christianity as a reforming

influence has indeed been slow, as men count slackness. But God has a great deal of time, and is never in a hurry. Consider the vast geological epochs which preceded the earth's arrival at its present form, — epochs computed not by thousands of years, but by hundreds of thousands. Consider the astronomical fact that nebulæ can be seen by Lord Rosse's telescope, the light of which has been millions of years in travelling the depths of space, — consequently nebulæ which we see as they were millions of years ago. Such facts should lift us in our reflections out of the limitations of our own short life. An ephemeral insect might be disappointed that in his long life of a whole summer's day men had made no more progress toward the completion of an edifice on which he made his home. So *we* complain, — human ephemera, — but receive the true solution of our doubts in the Apostle's words, "that with God a thousand years are as one day." Eighteen and a half centuries, therefore, have only brought us to the afternoon of the second day since the birth of Jesus. The question of slow or fast is one which we cannot moot in relation to the progress of Christianity. The only question is, Does Christianity really make progress? And in regard to that, how can there be any doubt? Its influence and advance in both the ways predicted by Jesus are apparent in human history. As the "leaven hid in the meal," an unseen influence pervading society, and as an institution small at first as "a grain of mustard-seed," but growing until the birds lodge in its branches, Christianity has determined the direction of all modern history. Modern history is the history of Christian civilization, and its characteristic feature is the progressive diffusion among the masses of the privileges formerly monopolized by the few. So, too, as an institution, it has developed itself first in the form of a Church, with outward unity, and a powerful hierarchy; next, in the form of a Creed; thirdly, as an inward Life of Piety; and is now advancing into its last great epoch of an outward life of Human Brotherhood.

Thus far, it is true, the Christian Church has not devoted itself with energy to the improvement of society, the removal of social evils, and the coming of God's kingdom in the world. It has been more interested in ecclesiastical questions, theological questions, and questions of experimental religion, than in those which regard morality and humanity. It has spent vast energy of thought upon questions of Church organization, of the Papacy, of the Episcopacy, of adult and infant baptism, of liturgies, and of sacraments. It has devoted itself with the utmost strain of thought, and outlay of learning, to the discussion of the doctrines of the Trinity, Human Depravity, the Divine Decrees, and the Atonement of Christ. It has used every effort to convert souls to God, to promote personal piety, to enlarge the borders of the Church, and to produce revivals of religion. But thus far it has done much less to remove pauperism, to reform criminals, to comfort the sick, to visit the prisoner, to save the victims of licentiousness, to prevent popular vices, to elevate the standard of education, to abolish slavery, to put a stop to war. These, no doubt, it ought to have done, without leaving the others undone.

One bad consequence of this one-sidedness in the action of the Church has been the production of a similar one-sidedness on the part of philanthropists. Because religion has been divorced from philanthropy, therefore morality is in turn divorced from religion. Earnest and conscientious men, looking at the evils of society, form associations for removing these evils by force of argument and discussion. Deeply convinced of the Christian character of these enterprises, and finding the Church indifferent to them and occupied only with works of piety, they denounce this indifference, and undervalue the works of piety in order to celebrate the works of philanthropy. And thus this unfortunate schism is perpetuated between the two departments of Christian life. And thus all humane efforts languish and stand still, for want of the powerful central influence which comes from piety.

For all the good works done in the past have been done by the power of Faith. This is the great lever by which man is moved, by which the world is lifted, and heaven is the place outside of earth where the philanthropists must stand to move this lever. Faith in God, in a special Providence, in an answer to Prayer, has given strength to the weak, and wrought wonders in the history of the world. Misdirected as to its end, it has manifested powers which, when rightly used, are adequate to change the whole face of society. That power of Faith which carried Christian Europe to faint on the hot sands of Syria, in order to recover the tomb where Christ's body was laid, will one day accomplish greater wonders in building the home where his spirit shall dwell. That power of faith which enabled the Maid of Arc, by her own force, to reverse the fortunes of war and to reconquer France, will nerve many another spirit, pure and true as hers, in nobler conquests over misery and sin. The power of Faith which in the thirteenth century covered Europe with magnificent cathedrals, which the present age may admire, but cannot rival, will erect more beautiful temples for divine worship, not of stone and wood, but of reformed institutions and an altered society. The power of Faith which brought the Mayflower to Plymouth harbor, bearing within its small cabin the founders of a great nation, will yet change and ennoble all our institutions, till they become those of a truly Christian commonwealth. It is the power of Faith and Prayer which will carry forward man in the sphere of moral and humane enterprise, as they have been the great motive powers in other places of religious life.

There stands a petition in the centre of the Christian's daily prayer, the sum and substance of all, being in itself both supplication and resolve, prophetic from the first of this divine union of piety and philanthropy, of faith and works, of love to God and love to man. When we say, "Thy kingdom come," our prayer is itself a prophecy of the second coming of Christ, and a means of accelerating it. And when we say,

"Thy will be done on earth," we not only ask for the reign of truth and love, but we devote ourselves to its establishment.

These words are inadequate for the settlement of the great question we have been considering. All words are inadequate. But every one who, longing for the reign of Christ, prays the prayer of faith, does something to settle the question. He knows in his own heart the power which comes from prayer, and he hastens the time when all prayer will be also work, because work will be its constant fruit and issue.

In looking forward to the days which are to come, when sincere and simple prayer shall thus fill every part of human life with beauty and joy, and bear rich fruit in all forms of righteousness; when the departments of Christian life shall be no more divided, but all in harmony; when the Church, being at one, can work without hinderance for the conversion of the world; and when man shall be like the orange-tree, "that busy plant," bearing at the same time foliage, flowers, and fruit, combining the fragrance of devotion with ripe results in action, — we may think of Jesus as still speaking to the world and saying, "Hitherto ye have asked NOTHING in my name; ASK AND RECEIVE, THAT YOUR JOY MAY BE FULL."

CHAPTER VII.

THE SPIRITUAL LIFE.

§ 44. *The Spiritual Life as the Source of Prayer.*

THE Doctrine of Prayer has been thus far treated by us in its various relations. This supplementary chapter will treat of the Spiritual Life, which is the perennial fountain of prayer. We shall consider first the soul itself, its nature and capacities; then treat of its hidden life, a life hid with Christ in God; then describe the natural man and the spiritual man in their discernment of things natural and spiritual; then speak of Sin and its confession and forgiveness; then of Assurance; and, lastly, of Contentment. We shall thus conclude our Essay with these general views of the Christian life, which will connect our idea of Prayer with all parts of the culture and discipline of the soul.

§ 45. *The Soul: its Nature and Capacities.*

Among the Jews, the soul was considered to be, not only the principle of thought, but also the principle of life. We, in our philosophy, follow the Romans, who regarded the thinking principle as one thing, and the principle of life as another. The Romans called the principle of thought MENS, whence comes our word *mental;* and the principle of life ANIMA, whence come our words *animation*, *animated*, as when we speak of the *animated creation*. But in the New Testament, one Greek word expresses the principle of bodily life, and of moral and intellectual power. According to this, it was the soul which kept the body alive. Some have gone further, and thought that the soul formed the body; and that there is a natural connection between each man's form and face, and the character of the soul; as when Spenser says,

> "For of the *soul* the body *form* doth take,
> For soul IS FORM, and doth the body make."

Which of these views is correct, I shall not now inquire. It was necessary to mention them, that we may understand that, when the words *life* and *soul* occur in the New Testament, the same Greek word is often used in the original.

But what is the soul, and what do we know about it? There is something in man which is especially himself, and which he means whenever he says "I." Of this something which we call "I," "Me," "Myself," we know certainly thus much: — *First*, that it exists. *Second*, that it thinks, feels, resolves, and carries out its volitions by moving the body. *Thirdly*, we know that it is one, — an absolute unit. It is one and the same thing which sees, hears, feels, thinks, resolves, acts, remembers the past, looks forward to the future, enjoys or suffers in the present. In this respect we immediately see a difference between the soul and the body. The body is an aggregate of different parts or organs, and its unity is not *simple* unity, but *compound* unity. With one part of the body, we see; with another, hear; with a third, taste; and so on. Not so with the soul. It is the same thing which sees, which hears, which tastes; and also which thinks, loves, chooses. Moreover, in the *fourth* place, we know that the soul is a substance; that is, something permanent, remaining the same thing amid change. For we know that it is the same thing which just now felt, or thought, or listened; and which now remembers, observes, or considers.

Thus much, then, we know. To all this we

have the testimony of our consciousness. What we have stated is not speculation, but certainty. We are certain of our own *existence*, as a *single, thinking and feeling, permanent substance* or *being*. This self we call the Soul. That is the name which men have agreed upon. If they should agree to call it the body, that would not change any of these facts which I have now stated, and of which my readers are just as certain as I am.

What shall we say, then, to those who assert that the soul is the body? — materialists, as they call themselves. Merely that they make an improper use of language. If they say that the soul is material, then they must assert that there is a peculiar kind of matter which has the power of thinking, feeling, and choosing, — a kind of matter, the qualities of which are not perceived through the senses, — a kind of matter which is indivisible, without parts, an absolute unit. Now this description is the precise opposite to all usual definitions of matter; for the common definition of matter is, That which is perceived through the senses; which is divisible; which has parts, and so on. Now to call two things, which are characterized by exactly opposite qualities, by the same name, seems an improper use of language.

Of this substance — the soul — it is true we know nothing except its qualities, — that it thinks, feels, and so forth. But the same thing is true of that other substance, body. All we know of this is its qualities, as color, form, extension, resistance, divisibility, and so on. When we perceive color, form, resistance, we infer by a necessary law of the mind that there is something colored, hard, and the like. We perceive these sensible qualities, and infer material substance. So when we perceive thought and feeling by means of our consciousness, we infer, by a necessary law of the mind, that there is something which thinks and feels. We perceive these mental qualities, and infer an immaterial substance. We call it immaterial, to indicate that its qualities are the precise opposite to those of matter.

That the soul stands in close connection with matter, while united with the body, we admit. It may always stand in close connection with matter. That mental qualities and states greatly depend upon bodily qualities and states, we also admit. This, too, may be always the case, for all that we know. But to be connected with a thing, and to be dependent upon a thing, is by no means equal to being identical with it. The trunk of a tree depends upon the root, and the fruit depends upon the twig, and they cannot exist apart; but that does not prove them to be the same thing.

I have now told all that I know with certainty about the soul. Beyond this comes a region of belief; and further out still, a region of opinion; and still further, one of speculation. To these frontier-settlements and remote hunting-grounds of the intellect, I do not propose to carry my readers. We have journeyed thus far through a land of certainties.

§ 46. *The Value of the Soul, shown by Five Arguments.*

If this is the soul, we ask, in the next place, What is its worth? What is its real value? I do not mean merely what is its value to ourselves, but, What is its value to the universe? What is its value in the eyes of God?

To answer this question, it is necessary to consider more particularly the qualities of the soul, — its powers and attributes. One of these is that of growth, development, and progress. Of this growth or development, the vegetable and animal world is an outward, visible symbol. Unorganized matter passes through changes and chemical transformation; but organized matter alone grows by a law of development. In every seed there lies hidden the law of especial development. Every seed is to have its own body. You plant an acorn in the ground, and you are sure that, if it becomes a tree, that tree will possess a certain kind of wood, bark, leaves, flowers, and fruit. Why is it that, among the trees which spring from a million acorns, not a single tree should have among its million leaves a single leaf with the indentation or form of that of a chestnut or walnut? Through all centuries, these seeds obey each its own law of development.

A similar law, of which this is the symbol, is connected with the soul of man. As every seed has its own body, so every soul has its own law of development, — of growth. Each one of us is intended by God for a special end. Each one of us is meant to grow according to the law of his own nature. Each one has capacities of development which this mortal life cannot reveal, much less exhaust. Who knows, who can imagine, what is hidden in the soul of each one of us? In the great men of the world we see hints of what all men are intended to become and surpass. A Newton, measuring the planets; a Herschel, numbering the stars; a Bacon, examining the powers of the human mind; a Shakespere, Dante, Milton, Homer, exhausting worlds, and then imagining new ones; an Alfred, or Washington, making himself the father of a nation; a Luther, arousing the human race with the great idea of freedom; a peasant-girl going, like Joan of Arc, to save her country from the conquering armies of invaders, and saving it; a Kossuth, carrying the sorrows of his people in his heart from land to land, and pleading for them as if the woes and wrongs of all spoke in his generous voice; a Socrates, consuming the last hours of a well-spent life in cheerful discourse, which foretells his future immortality by its spirit more than its arguments, as the glories of the setting sun are ominous of a clear to-morrow; — what are all these manifestations of human nature, but indications to us of powers which lie in every bosom? They speak of the inherent powers, of the native greatness, of every soul. Were it not so, how could we understand them, — why should we admire them? The eloquence of true nobleness finds an echo in all our hearts. The sympathy which stirs in every soul toward great thoughts, great endeavors, great self-devotion, is the movement of a kindred power stirring within us, and asking room for a like development. When you strike a harp-string, every other harp-string in the room which is set to the same chord responds. When any human faculty greatly expresses itself, the same faculty hid in myriad hearts responds by a thrill of admiring sympathy.

Again, the worth of the soul appears in its capacities, because these capacities are divine. A sentence full of meaning stands at the beginning of the Old Testament, — "In the image of God created he man." Our power of knowing God depends on our being made in his image. We ascribe to him the attributes of omniscience, omnipotence, omnipresence, and perfect goodness. These words would convey no meaning to us, if there were not in each soul similar *finite* capacities. We have within us ideas of truth, of right, of holiness, knowledge, power, love. We have also the idea of the infinite, the independent, the eternal. These ideas belong to the constitution of the human soul. By means of them we know God, without them we could have no knowledge of him. The worth of the soul appears in this, then, that it is thus made in the image of God. For these ideas are native and original to the soul. They lie in the texture of every soul. They may be darkened by sin ; they may be hidden by ignorance or error ; but they are there. A worldly life may conceal them, as the shadow of the earth eclipses the moon, but the moon is there, though its pure, bright light is changed and dimmed. So earthly mists may altogether hide the stars, but the mist drifts away when God's pure wind blows, and the stars appear again in their old, eternal homes. They were hidden for a while, but they were always there.

Again, the worth of the soul appears from the fact, that it may be the temple of God. In all ages man has built his noblest and most beautiful edifices for the worship of God. Amid the eternal solitudes of Thebes still remain the immense rows of columns, miles in length, through which the priestly procession once marched in solemn pomp. At Balbec the impostal stones of immense size, some sixty feet long, are still supported in the air. The most beautiful work of art which man has ever built was the Temple for the worship of Minerva at Athens. The Temple of the Sun at Palmyra in the wilderness, the caves of Elephanta in India, the pagodas in Birmah and China, the ruins of Palenque in Central America, the vast stones at Stonehenge in England, the remains of the Jewish Temple at Jerusalem, and the Pantheon at Rome, are all proofs that man exerts his best power and genius in building for the worship of God. But God dwells not in temples made with hands. The numan soul he has made for his temple, and there he desires to dwell. He dwells in the heart purified by love. The music to which he listens is the melody of grateful affection. The incense of praise is the perfume which rises acceptably to him. In that temple the sermons are the thoughts inspired by God's own spirit; the prayers are the aspirations of the soul after truth and holiness; the acceptable worship is the spirit of Christ.

Again, the worth of the soul is seen in what God has done to redeem it from sin, and to prepare it for immortality. The world itself, with all its contents, the whole apparatus of earthly life, with its joys and its trials, its labor and repose, its conflicts and vicissitudes, — for what else was it intended, but to develop and educate human life and human souls? This purpose alone makes human life and human destiny intelligible. Other purposes there may also be; for who can limit the Divine Providence? But this alone is to us intelligible. We can understand a little of the mystery of evil, when we see that evil tends to strengthen and educate the soul. We can comprehend something of the tangled skein of history, when we see the gradual progress wrought out in the culture of races and individuals, and all human history preparing the way for Christ. And, finally, in Christianity itself we see most plainly how God values the soul, — valuing it, not according to its present attainments, but according to its inherent capacities; having more joy in the one sinner that repents, than in the ninety-and-nine just persons who need no repentance. The goodness of the best man is nothing, compared with the goodness which the worst man is capable of attaining. This is a point in Christianity which we are slow to comprehend. We overvalue present attainment; we undervalue inherent capability. The small house suited to our present convenience, and finished in a year, we value more than the vast palace, the enormous cathedral, the metropolitan city, whose great plan it will require centuries to execute. Esau, selling his birthright for a mess of pottage, is the type of those who despise the common human nature which is in every man, and idolize the talents of this or that brilliant person, here or there.

Jesus did not so. Jesus reverenced the great nature which he saw in the soul of every man. Therefore he reverenced the child whose unpolluted soul still beheld the face of God. Therefore he looked with tenderness on the sinner, — spoke words of loftiest truth to the most humble and called upon the common crowd to be perfect, as their Father in heaven was perfect. Therefore he demanded of all, as the only essential thing, to turn their faces the right way in faith, to have courage, to believe in God and in themselves. In this conception of the possibilities of man, the roots of all great Christian ideas find nourishment. Love to God is strengthened when our love is not abject, but hopeful, flowing from the consciousness of what he has made us to be. Love to man is possible only when we see in every man the capacity of goodness, beauty, and power. We can love the sinner when the actual sin appears superficial, and the possible goodness radical. We can forgive an enemy when we see that this enemy, by means of our forgiveness, may not only become our friend, but the friend of God. We can look on ourselves with humility and yet with hope, on the prosperous without envy, on the sufferer without too sickly a sorrow, on our trials with patience, and our successes without elation, when we consider how little all these things are in comparison with the universal soul which is in all, with its boundless capacities, with its glorious destiny.

And this destiny of the soul is the last proof of its greatness to which I would refer. There is, in the New Testament, a doctrine which has been much perverted and misunderstood, but which, when rightly viewed, is full of inspiration and encouragement. It is the doctrine of predestination; which I would rather call the doctrine of destination, as we can conceive no before or after with God. As all things are present to God, he neither foreknows nor predetermines anything, but knows and determines everything, — our own choice and the Divine decree co-operating in every act. Nevertheless, in human language we must speak of God's foreknowledge and predestination. Now, the doctrine of the New Testament is, that before the foundation of the world, God determined our destiny. *How* is not there stated. But it may be that it was by giving to each one of us a special nature and capacity, making each separate soul an individual unit, and arranging for each one the outward circumstances and events of our earthly life. It is no accident, but the Divine decree, which has made us just the beings that we are. He chose us to be such before the foundation of the world. He destined us in love to be adopted as children, through Jesus Christ, and brought to the heart of our Father. Everything, therefore, in our constitution, organization, and circumstances, has a divine meaning; and that, a meaning of love. Every man is made for a special place and a special work, — a place which no other man can fill, a work which no other man can do. Some are made for a higher, and some for a lower work, but every work is divine. There is a great order in the universe; and some are made to be greater, wiser, more powerful, more useful, glorious, and happy, than others; but all are made to be equally children of God, equally near to their Father's heart. All is part of one system, and in that system nothing is insignificant. (The greatest events in human history apparently depend on the smallest circumstances.) A ray of sunlight breaking from the clouds and shining in the face, dazzling the eyes of an army, changed the issue of one of the great battles which have been turning-points in the destinies of our race. The safe arrival of a missionary, destined to convert a continent, may depend on the accuracy of a chronometer, which accuracy depends on the right adjustment of the smallest pin or screw. So, in God's universe, the most insignificant soul may be most significant, — essential to the happiness of all. Every wilfulness or sin of ours may interfere with the bliss of angels, and darken the light of heaven. God is glorified when we bear fruit. When we are faithful, we hasten by so much the great consummation of all things; when unfaithful, we retard by so much the redemption of the world. When faithful, we are at one with all the pure and good in all worlds, — heirs of God, and joint heirs with Christ. In every moment of such fidelity is fulfilled for us the great promise, "All things are yours, whether prophets or apostles, life or death, things present or things to come." Thus each soul is destined for a growth and progress which shall, at the same time, develop more and more his individual personal character, and unite him more and more with all other beings; which shall make him more entirely himself, and shall unite him more entirely with the whole. Thus shall result, at last, that great concert of the universe, where each individual contributes a single note of music which, distinct in itself, yet in harmony with the rest, makes up the music of the spheres.

§ 47. *The Soul's Hidden Life.*

"Your life is hid with Christ in God." These are the words, not of the mystical, but of the logical Apostle. They lead us forward, from the view just taken of the nature of the soul, to its new life hidden in Christ. This is the essence of Christianity. Life, inward and hidden, the source of the public and open life, is the one thing needful to us all. I will go on to describe this hidden spiritual life, and to show that there must be such a life "hid with Christ in God." Christianity does not consist in action only. There must be something beside the act, and behind it, as its source. And this source of religion is something secret and hidden, — hidden in the depths of the soul. The river which rolls its sparkling waters in the light of day, has its dark fountains, hidden below the surface, somewhere. The plant, which spreads its leaves and hangs its flowers in the cheerful sunlight, has a root hidden below the soil. And you might as well expect to find a river with its springs above ground, or a plant with its roots all bare, as true religion without a secret, untold, and inexplicable source in the depths of the soul. The root of religion consists in deep convictions and profound feelings, — in convictions of God's presence, of personal accountability, of a judgment to come, of God's tender love to us, of the beauty of holiness in Jesus Christ, — feelings which no words can fully express, no actions exhaust. The most fervid eloquence, the most rapt devotion, must fall far short of unfolding the feeling which prompts it.

There must be more behind than is told. There is more love in the heart than can look out at the eye. All language must be inadequate to express the religious sentiment. The root may shoot forth from the ground, but the root itself must stay below. Far as the river runs, it never brings the spring out after it into the air. That must stay behind. In the same way, as long as a man's religion is genuine and living, so long must there be a secret source to it. If, then, one is not conscious of feeling more than he can say,— if he has no private thoughts and secret feelings, unuttered and unutterable, — then his religion has no root within; it is not his at all; it is a superficial, hearsay, borrowed thing, which he has picked up by the way-side; it is a traditional, and not a personal affair; flesh and blood have revealed it to him, and not his Father in heaven. The spirit of God has not breathed it into his soul, but the words of man have taught it to his intellect. It is a vanity, a nothing. If a man, then, has no *secret* religion, he has no religion.

If there were any doubt about the truth of this, it would be made certain by the fact, that the same thing is true, in a less degree, of all our other convictions, all our other belief. If a man merely receives an opinion from another, and his own mind does not act upon it, work it over, look at it, and make it his own by reflection, it is not *his* opinion; it does not belong to him yet; it belongs to the man from whom he took it. But if he does ruminate it and digest it in his own mind, this is a hidden process which he never can fully explain to himself or any one else.

§ 48. *A Hidden Life the Evidence of Sincerity.*

Again. A hidden life is necessary as an evidence of sincerity.

If a man finds that he loves to talk about religion a great deal more than to think about it, he ought to fear lest his supposed love for truth is partly a love for hearing himself talk, and for having others admire his fine sentiments. If he finds that secret prayer is not so agreeable as to conduct devotions at a prayer-meeting, or to join audibly in the responses at church, there is danger that he loves the reputation of religion more than its reality. If he perceives that, while he is ready to put his name on a subscription-paper, or his money into a contribution-box, he has not given much in secret charity, he should dread lest he has been seeking the reputation of generosity, or avoiding the reproach of others, instead of being desirous of doing good and relieving misery. If he goes to church or avoids working on the Lord's day, or abstains from any gratification, or shows a respect to religion only for the sake of example, he should consider that to recommend a thing to others which we do not care about ourselves is hardly treating them fairly. If, in the trying circumstances of life, the conflicts of opinion, the temptations to swerve a little way from duty, he never steps aside to look at the divine standard of virtue, to ask what is right in itself and for ever, not what men think right, or what is fashionable *now* and *here*, — if he never endeavors to free himself from the influence of a worldly morality and the examples of the times to look at the pure morality of Jesus Christ by which he and all are to be judged, — he ought to be very anxious lest he be not wishing to know what is right at all, but only what is popular; not wishing to do what is right at all, but only to do what is convenient and easy. Or if a man professing to be a disciple of Christ finds himself lazily acquiescing in the views of the majority with regard to Christian doctrine, never testing his creed by Scripture nor by reason, never trying the spirits to see whether they be of God, he ought to suspect that he is not the disciple of Christ, but the disciple of Calvin, of Wesley, of

Priestley, and that his true place is not in the Protestant, but the Romish Church. But on the other hand, if he can say that he has sought earnestly to know the truth as it is in Jesus Christ, that he has endeavored to govern his conduct by a rule and motives not of this world, that his opinions and feelings are not the mere reflection of those of others, that his mind is something more than a camera obscura containing only the picture of what is going on about him, that his life is not the mere sport of external influences and circumstances, but that he has an inward life of personal convictions, principles, purposes, rooted deep in his soul, — if he perceives that his faith is dear to him, though unpopular, that religion is a comfort to him in his secret trials, that he feeds on hidden manna, and has a joy with which the stranger does not intermeddle, — if the words which he sometimes utters in behalf of God and truth are the overflow of a full vessel, the gushing out of a swelling heart, — if he enjoys doing good though no one knows of it, and finds a satisfaction in righteousness, even though misunderstood and misrepresented, his good be evil spoken of, — if he can calmly bear false accusations, and patiently endure calumny, — then he may be at least certain that vanity and display are not among the motives which actuate him; he may be as sure as we can be in this world, where we see everything through a glass and darkly, even our own hearts, that his purposes are sincere and his piety genuine. And with this conviction, what more can he wish?

§ 49. *The Hidden Life known to God.*

Again. It is unquestionable that we *must* have a hidden life of some kind, either good or bad; the only question is, which shall it be? If we do not watch over our inward nature, attend to the motives which actuate us, cherish good feelings, keep our heart with diligence, — if we neglect altogether what is going on in our souls, and fix our thoughts only on external things, and endeavor to lose ourselves in the enjoyments and pursuits of the outward world, — we do not thereby destroy the world within us. There is still a whole secret world there of thoughts, and purposes, and wishes, perpetually going on. Because we do not choose to think of it or look at it, we do not annihilate it. Every man that lives must live a double life, — a life of outward action and a life of inward feeling and motive. The only question then is, whether he shall attend to this inward life and watch it and make it a pure one, or whether he shall let it go on becoming more and more corrupt and foul, till the light of God's judgment comes, in the words of an apostle, " to judge the secrets of men by Jesus Christ."

This is the true question; not whether we shall have a hidden life, but whether we shall neglect it and try to forget what is within, looking not at the things unseen and eternal, but at those seen and temporal, — whether we shall suffer the inward man to perish day by day, or strive to make it more pure day by day. The question is, whether our life shall be hidden from ourselves. For it cannot be hidden from God. His eye is ever open on our heart, and our soul is ever naked to him. He sets our secret sins in the light of his countenance. He writes every thought and purpose which we have, be it base or be it holy, in his book of remembrance. The hidden man of the heart he sees and will judge. O, is it not a wonderful thing, that we should labor so to disguise our faults, and hide our disgraces from the eye of the world; that we should shrink with such fear from letting our weaknesses be known to others; that we should strive so painfully to deceive ourselves, and persuade ourselves by all kinds of sophistry that we are pure; that we should take such pains to excuse and justify and palliate our faults, when we know that we cannot hide them from God, and that in a very few years they *must* be known to all?

Yes, there is nothing which is covered which shall not be revealed, nor anything hid which shall not be known. The day is coming which shall try every man's work, tear off every disguise, and show what men really are. In that day shall the hypocrites call on the rocks to cover them, and pray to be buried under the mountain avalanche; — yes, to be hid beneath the burning waves of the lake of fire, rather than to have their consciences and souls probed by the keen ray of truth. Ah! what a revelation shall there be on that day, when the Pharisees of every age come up to judgment, saying, "Lord! Lord! did we not prophesy in thy name, and in thy name cast out demons, and do all manner of wonderful works?" and then shall he profess unto them, "Depart from me, I never knew you, ye workers of iniquity." But they will say, "We were famous for our piety, we were noted for our devotion, we were of the strictest sect of orthodoxy, our names were in public charities." "Yes, but your hearts were full of selfishness and sin; you judged others, you never judged yourselves; you plucked the mote out of the eye of your neigh bor, you suffered the beam to remain in your own; you were bigoted, intolerant, uncharitable; you had not the spirit of Christ, you are none of his."

And in that day others shall come up, and hope to be saved because of their good works; and they shall say, "Lord, we were accounted just and good men; we paid our debts, we told the truth, we gave to the poor; no man can accuse us of any wrong." "Ah!" but the Lord will say, "your goodness was a shadow, it rested on the opinion of men; you wished to be popular, and to have the reputation of virtue and its advantages, but you never judged yourselves by any purer standard; you washed your hands, but you did not wash your hearts; your goodness was hollow and selfish, it had no root within; there was no deep conviction, no living faith, no real charity, in your souls; depart."

So shall it be with the self-deceivers and the hypocrites on that great and terrible day. But ye, pure children of God, who hungered and thirsted after real righteousness, who judged yourselves daily by the high standard of holiness, whose struggles and prayers and tears no man ever knew, whose secret acts and words of love were unrecorded by human pen, unuttered by human lips, blazoned on no stately monument ye who suffered wrong patiently, looking for a recompense hereafter; ye weak ones, thrust aside and trampled under foot by the men of this world. ye solitary ones, living in the by-ways and hedges of life, and offering your Master the two mites which was all that you had, bringing ointment to anoint his feet, when you could do no more for him, — ye shall not fail of your reward; your life is hid with Christ in God; but what is hid shall be known, and in the day when the paraded virtues of this world shall fade beneath the scorching beam of the great judgment, you shall sit on thrones and shine forth as the sun in the kingdom of the Father. The hypocrites and the hollow-hearted have had their reward; they loved the praise of man better than the praise of God, and they obtained it. They have had in their lifetime the good things they lusted after. They lived in the smooth element of plausibility, they were popular everywhere, for they took care never to run counter to any prevailing prejudice, never to lift up their voices against any prevailing sin. Rather they busied themselves in seeking arguments to protect sinful usages against the rebuke of Christ, and to rock asleep the half-awakened conscience by sweet songs of smooth morality. They were willing to

> "Torture the pages of the blessed Bible,
> To sanction crime, and robbery, and blood,
> And in oppression's hateful service libel
> Both man and God."

They told pleasant truths in a pleasant way, and of unpleasant ones they said nothing. These men were never found with the minority, struggling to open men's eyes to prevailing abuses; always in the self-complacent majority, willing to let everything remain as it was. And so they fell asleep amid the murmuring praises of a world always willing to praise those who let it go its own way unreproved; and so they were followed to their graves by pompous processions, and eulogies and harangues innumerable were uttered over them.

Otherwise was it in life with the man who carried his conscience into his conduct, and his heart on his lips. Otherwise was it with him; for him was ordained a burden of unsuccessful labor for truth; to be scouted at and ridiculed, and stoned and persecuted; to be misunderstood and misrepresented; to make, indeed, a few warm friends, but also many loud enemies; to be despised and rejected of men; or at best, never to have his sincere virtues appreciated, never to win popular applause or fame. He cared not for it, however; he went his own way; he knew the Lord was on his side; he knew that good men must be his friends, if not now, by and by. He spoke what seemed to him to be the truth, whether men would hear or whether they would forbear. He had delivered his own soul, and he left the rest to God.

> "He came, and, baring his heaven-bright thought,
> He earned the base world's ban;
> And, having vainly lived and taught,
> Gave place to a meaner man."

No pompous procession followed him to the narrow grave where he was laid to repose; but the faithful feet of those whom he had comforted and taught and strengthened sought it day by day,

> "And childhood's tears, like summer rain,
> Quickened its dying grass again."

And so they lie, side by side, the plausible man of the world and the man whose life was hid with Christ in God. So they lie, waiting for the resurrection.

§ 50. *The Natural Man does not discern Spiritual Truth.*

The saying of the Apostle, that "the natural man receiveth not the things of the spirit of God, for they are foolishness unto him; neither can he know them, for they are spiritually discerned," — has been thought to be difficult and made difficult; nevertheless, it is in itself perfectly simple and intelligible.

When a doctrine is preached which seems contradictory to reason and common sense, and we object to it on that ground, we are often told that it is our carnal reason which is offended, and then this text is quoted, as though it meant, "No one who has not been miraculously converted can comprehend the doctrines of Christianity."

But to this view there are serious objections. If we cannot understand Christian doctrines until we are converted, it would seem to follow, that we never can understand them at all. For these doctrines contain the very truth which is intended to convert us, and except we understand that truth, it can have no power over us. The doctrines of Christianity are intended to bring men to repentance; but except they are understood, they can never produce this result.

If, therefore, this explanation is not the true one, what is the real meaning of the passage?

It is usual for preachers to divide men into two classes, the converted and the unconverted, the penitent and the impenitent, the saints and the sinners. And no doubt there is a foundation for this distinction. But the Scripture also divides men into three classes, according to its threefold distinction of man into Spirit, Soul, and Body. This distinction, almost universal in ancient times, considered man in his central, essential being as A SOUL; finite, individual; a pure unit, or monad; indivisible, and containing in itself personal identity. This soul, or *Psyche*, the central element in man, is connected by the spirit with eternity and God, by the body with sense and time. Now "*the spiritual man*" is he whose soul is turned, through the spirit, to eternity and heaven. The carnal man is he whose soul is turned, through the body, to sensual gratification. But besides these two positions, there is a third, namely, that of the man who is neither carnal nor spiritual,—not immersed in appetite, nor conversant with God, or eternal truth. Such a man is called, in the New Testament language, the *natural man;* in the original, the *psychical* or *soul man.* This man's position is that of the great majority of human beings. They are not religious, they are not sensual. They occupy, therefore, that middle ground, which, for want of a better name, we call worldliness. Their purposes, occupations, and enjoyments are all worldly, limited to the present life. There is nothing necessarily vicious in their conduct. They conform, in outward behavior and inward purpose, to the worldly standard of morality and propriety. They are not infidels. They willingly receive Christianity as a divine revelation. But practically they are controlled by worldly ideas; practically, Christ is not their king, God not in their thoughts, eternity and heaven are things impalpable and afar off. While the *spiritual man* believes spiritual truth, loves spiritual happiness, and pursues spiritual improvement, and while *the carnal man* believes in material things, enjoys sensual gratification, and labors for sensual happiness, the *natural or worldly man* is guided in his mind by the opinions of the world, loves in his heart the honors and successes of the world, and makes it the object of his efforts to obtain them.

The assertion of the Apostle, therefore, is this: that the worldly man, who is leading a worldly life, is unable, while in this state of mind, to see the reality of spiritual things; that they must seem to him foolish, impracticable, and visionary; and that the only way to discern them is by means of spiritual experience. In other words, the worldly man cannot, by means of mere intellect, know God or believe in Christ, or heartily accept the truths of the Gospel. He asserts, therefore, that a spiritual preparation is necessary in order to discern spiritual truth. Now I shall endeavor to show that this doctrine is unobjectionable, because it accords with common sense and the laws of human nature; that it is certain, because it accords with experience; and that it is a truth of the greatest importance in its various applications.

This doctrine accords with common sense, and the laws of human nature. Common sense teaches that every kind of truth has its appropriate evidence. Thus there are truths of the material universe, and their appropriate evidence is the experience of the senses. This evidence, again, is subdivided. The appropriate evidence of visible things is sight; of tangible things, touch; of audible things, hearing; and so forth.

Now suppose a man should say, "I will not believe in the *sun*, unless I can touch it; I will not believe in the wind, unless I can see it; I will not believe that the rose has perfume, unless I can taste it; I will not believe in the sound of a cannon, unless I can hold it in my hand." "Why," you would say to him, "you demand, sir, an inappropriate kind of evidence, and you cannot have it. A sound must be audibly discerned; an object of sight must be optically discerned."

Again, there are mathematical and logical truths, and these are discerned by demonstration or deduction. Thus the truth, that the three angles of a triangle are equal to two right angles, cannot be discerned optically, or audibly, but logically. We cannot taste, touch, or smell this truth, we know it by a process of reasoning. Yet we are perfectly sure of it, and the lives and property of thousands are risked every year on the truth of it.

Other things are proved or discerned by *testimony*. Thus we all know that there is such a place as St. Petersburg; we know it so well, that we would risk our life on the certainty of its existence. Yet we know it, not by sensible evidence, for we have never seen it; nor by logical evidence, for we could not reason out its existence. We know it by the testimony of those who have seen it. Just so we believe in the existence of Julius Cæsar, or in the facts of the life of Jesus. We believe them by a chain (or rather a web) of testimony.

Other truths, again, are discerned by means of consciousness or intuition; for example, our own existence. We cannot touch it or taste it. We cannot prove it logically or mathematically, we cannot know it through the testimony of others. We discern it intuitively. So likewise it is with the other emotions and conceptions of the human mind, with love, hope, fear, choice, effort, justice; we know all these, and distinguish them from each other, intuitively, — by an inward sight.

If, therefore, there is a material world, the truths of which are discerned by the senses, and only so; if there are logical and mathematical truths, which can only be discerned by demonstration; if there are historical truths, which can only be known by human testimony; if there are moral facts and truths, which can only be discerned intuitively by the moral consciousness, — it is quite in accordance with common sense, and the laws of human nature, that there should be spiritual truths, to be discerned spiritually. It is quite natural that those who do not *exercise* their spiritual nature should be incapable of perceiving the facts of the spiritual world.

For beside this law, that every kind of truth

has its own special organ by which it is discerned, there is another law, namely, that these organs must be exercised, in order to perform their function. The senses are continually exercised, and therefore they perform their functions sufficiently. But for finer observations, a special exercise is necessary. A sailor sees a ship on the horizon, where a landsman can see nothing. No one can understand the truths contained in a mathematical or metaphysical work, without having exercised his logical faculty. Our faith in human testimony, and in that of consciousness, is necessarily in constant exercise, and therefore it enables us to receive and to discern these truths.

And as regards the truths of the spiritual world, the case is the same. We are not compelled by the necessities of life to commune with God and immortality, and therefore these spiritual faculties may remain unexercised. If they are thus unexercised, we shall not be able to discern spiritual things. Such is the common law of all our faculties, and there is no reason to think that it will fail in this case. That it does not fail we shall now show. We shall show that a worldly man does not, as a matter of fact, see spiritual things, and that when he talks of them, he is like a blind man describing a landscape, or a deaf man giving an account of a concert.

The natural or worldly man cannot discern God. He can believe in God, or rather he can believe that there is a God on grounds of inference. This is the sort of belief produced by the study of natural theology. It is good so far as it goes. But it is a cold, lifeless, and unproductive belief. A man born blind may believe that there is beauty in outward nature, in the face of man, in drifting clouds and falling water, in the smile of affection and the light filling the eyes of genius. On grounds of testimony he may be quite sure of it; but will this belief be to him a source of joy and strength, as to those who can discern it all? The belief of the worldly man in God, is like this blind man's belief in a visible world. It is quite consistent with practical atheism. He is living without God, and therefore he does not discern God. He does not discern God in the world, for he does not look for God in the world. The world is to him a place where he can make money, and win triumphs, enjoy pleasure, and meet with outward success. He fixes his eye on all its arrangements and combinations for these purposes, and therefore does not see the great God behind them.

The human eye is so constituted, that it can see what is near to it, or that which is distant. In looking at a landscape, we may look at the foreground, and so not see the background, or we can look at the distant horizon, and so comprehend the whole. We may look through a glass at the distant heavens, or we may make the glass itself the focal point of vision, and so see nothing else. Now the world is such a glass. The devout man looks through it and sees God; the worldly man sees only the glass itself. For we have the power of fixing the eye of the soul so exclusively upon the things seen and temporal, that we shall not discern anything of the awful eternity behind them. This the worldly man does, and so becomes a practical atheist, living without God. He does not see God in nature, he sees only a dead machine, ingeniously put together long ago, and left by its maker to grind out what results it may with its iron mechanism. He sees no God in events, but only a hard necessity or an unmeaning tangle of accidents. They came from nothing; they tend nowhere. He sees no God in his trials or his blessings. He thanks himself, and not God, for his successes, he curses his bad luck for his losses. He sees no God in his human brethren; they are animals, creatures of appetite and selfishness. It were folly to try to do them good. Such a man is incapable of generous enthusiasm for right, of generous indignation at wrong; incapable of the inspiration coming from a far-reaching hope, or a high devotedness to duty. For it is only the sight of the infinite element which can awaken such an enthusiasm. His world is no Switzerland, where mountains soar aloft, piercing the sky with silver peaks, where icy rivers roll down their ravines, and the voice of the avalanche speaks in thunder above; but it is a monotonous Holland, good for cultivation, well fitted to produce cattle and potatoes, but nothing more.

Nor can the natural man discern Christ any more than God. He may be a firm believer in Christ as an historical and supernatural person. He may believe his miracles, every one of them, and may "deal damnation round the land" at every doubting Thomas, who has his difficulties on the subject. He may know Christ according to the flesh; but Christ according to the spirit, the real and true Christ, he cannot discern. The one condition of knowing Christ is willingness to follow him. The rule holds still, "How can ye believe who receive honor one from another, and not the honor which comes from God only?"

The sagacious and learned gentlemen at Jerusalem could not possibly discern their coming Messiah in Jesus of Nazareth, for he did not belong to their circles, — he was a mechanic poorly dressed, and talked what seemed to them radicalism, democracy, and atheism. We also find the same difficulty. We have surrounded Christ with a halo of glory, worship him as God, make him our Saviour in a future life, and think to follow him by going to church, and partaking of sacraments. And so we do not see the real Christ at all, — the friend of the poor and wretched, whose only business in this world is to lift the fallen and comfort the discouraged, to manifest God as a father to the sinner, and to denounce all selfishness as on the way to the damnation of hell. And so it happens that people, thinking themselves Christians, can make it their business in life to make money, to make power, reputation, knowledge for themselves, instead of gaining the talent in order to use it for others. Thus the great mass of nominal Christians do not discern the true Christ, the friend of man, who taught us to love our neighbor as ourselves.

Again, the natural or worldly man cannot discern the essential thing in Christianity; that is, its spiritual power, — its faith, hope, and love, — its inward life, hid in the soul, making us strong, peaceful, and true. These things must be spiritually discerned, and the spiritual organ, by which they are seen, is not yet developed in the mind of the natural man. To him they must seem like mysticism, enthusiasm, fanaticism, and folly. To him the essential thing in Christianity is not its spiritual part, its soul; but its outward body, its creeds and ceremonies. He conceives a man to be a Christian who accepts certain doctrines, and goes through certain external ceremonies. If a man believes an orthodox creed, goes to church, and partakes of the Lord's supper, he holds him to be, in all senses, a Christian, provided his outward conduct be also decent, and he keeps himself out of the hands of the police. He considers it the object of Christianity to save us from punishment in the future life, rather than from sin in the present life. Faith to him is the intellectual reception of certain doctrines; hope, the expectation of escaping punishment hereafter; and love, some pious emotion of satisfaction in being saved one's self, while others are lost. Such is the view which the worldly man naturally takes of the substance of Christianity. Having no spiritual tastes or sympathies, he has no means of seeing its interior nature. The outside only attracts him.

Finally, the worldly man cannot discern immortality, for that also must be spiritually discerned. He accepts the fact of a future life, but it does not take hold of him as a reality, because he does not let it influence his present course. If he lived for eternity, he would then feel the eternal world always near. But he lives for time, and therefore knows nothing beyond. When he lays his friends' bodies in the earth, it is as though he had buried *them*. They are wholly lost to him. In the trials of life it is no comfort to him to think of the happy land beyond, with its deeper insight, its higher aspiration, its larger, tenderer love, its profound peace, — the land of reunions, where all tears are wiped away, where anxieties, cares, and weighty responsibilities cease, where Christ shall be the nearest friend, and the presence of God a surrounding sunlight. Death is to him king of terrors, associated with coffins, black dresses, tombs, and desolation; not the angel with golden key, to unlock the low portal through which we step into larger liberty and life.

I have endeavored to show that it is not by the intellectual faculty, however keen and clear, that we perceive the things of the spiritual world. There is a way by which they can become visible and real to us, and thus the source of life and joy. It is by being willing to do God's will, and making it ours, that we become able to see them. They are spiritually discerned. He whose heart is pure sees God. He who loves goodness sees Christ. He who desires to do his will knows of the doctrine. He who lives here in this spirit has eternal life abiding in him, is in eternity and heaven now, and does not merely believe in immortality, but *knows* it. In nature he sees God; in the events of history he sees Providence; in sorrow and bereavement he sees a coming good; in the letter of the Bible he sees its holy spirit; and in the hour of death, he sees through its clouds and shadows the heavens open, and the Son of Man standing at the right hand of the throne of God.

§ 51. *Nature of Sin, and the Absence of a Sense of Sin.*

There is a remarkable passage in the First Epistle of John, which asserts, "If we say that we have no sin, we deceive ourselves, and the truth is not in us." This passage is interesting, but contains difficulties; and it is none the less interesting on account of these difficulties. A passage which contains no difficulty, contains little that we do not know already. When we meet with a verse in the New Testament which seems to contradict other places, or to be opposed to well-known facts, or to our opinions and experience, we may regard such a text as a field with treasure hid in it. That is the place where we are to dig, and where our labor will be rewarded by finding something which will be new to us. Let us beware how we explain away such a difficulty. Let us keep clear of any explanation commencing with the formula, "It only means" this or that. Let us expect that it will mean something important, and dig deep till we find it, or see that we are unable to find it.

The difficulty in this passage is in regard to a matter of fact.

"If we say that we have no sin." This implies that we do say so, at any rate sometimes; that we are either in the habit of saying so, or that we are in danger of saying so. But is this *a fact*? Does any one ever say, "I have no sin"? Do we not all admit that we are sinners, that we have often done wrong, that we are quite imperfect? Perhaps the majority of persons will admit, that, theologically speaking, they are totally depraved, in the theological sense nothing but sin. They will admit this very cheerfully and good-naturedly. I do not know that I ever met a man who denied that he was a sinner. I believe that almost every one admits that he offends, in many things, against the law of right. Hence it would seem that the Apostle is mistaken in the matter of fact, in implying that any one denies that he is a sinner. Here is a difficulty in the passage. Perhaps we may get its true explanation, by asking what the Apostle means by the word *sin.* If by sin he means one thing and we mean another, then, when we say that we are sinners in our sense of the word, we may nevertheless deny that we are sinners in his sense of the word. What, therefore, do *we* mean by sin, and what did the *Apostle* mean?

"Sin," says the New Testament, "is the transgression of the law." But what law? There are various kinds of law. There is, for example, *the law of the land*, which forbids those outward actions which interfere with the rights of our neighbor; which forbids and punishes offences against person and property; which forbids murder and theft, and the lower forms of these offences, — assault and battery, breach of trust, cheating, obtaining money by false pretences, and the like. It also forbids gross injury done with the tongue or pen, libel and slander, which inflict damage on a person in his character, personal or social. All these offences, punishable by the law of the land, are properly called *crimes*.

Then there are *constitutional and organic laws* of human nature, — laws written by God in the physical constitution of man, — laws which command sobriety, which forbid excess, which punish intemperance by disease. An offence against these laws we call *vice*. It is an offence committed directly against one's own physical well-being, and indirectly against the peace and welfare of society. These offences, however, are not often punished by the law of the land, although the amount of injury done to society by *vice* is far greater than that which is done by *crime*.

Next comes *the law of public opinion*, — a law varying in every community, according to its intelligence and morality, requiring and forbidding more in one place than in another, but everywhere requiring and forbidding more than either of the other laws. Public opinion, in every community, frowns upon actions which are not crimes against the state, nor vices against the person. A man who commits neither vice nor crime may be avaricious, hard-hearted, brutal, insincere, careless, ill-tempered, and so be condemned by public opinion. Offences against this law we will call *improprieties*. The conduct of the man who commits them may be neither criminal nor vicious, but it is improper.

Next comes the *law of conscience*, varying in every man according to his knowledge and culture, but usually requiring more and forbidding more than any of the others hitherto mentioned. A man may satisfy the law of the land, he may not offend the physical laws of his own constitution, he may satisfy the law of public opinion, and yet not satisfy himself. He commits neither crime, nor vice, nor impropriety, but he offends his own conscience, he violates his own resolutions and purposes, he does not come up to his own idea of duty.

Now this violation of the standard of right is what people usually mean when they say that they are sinners. They do not quite come up to their own ideal. They fall short of what their own reason and sense of right demand of them. They do something, but they ought to do more. By sin, therefore, they mean IMPERFECTION.

But was this all that the Apostle meant by sin? I think he meant more. It was not merely the violation of the law of conscience, which demands improvement, but of the Christian law, which demands love, — of that law which says, "Thou shalt love the Lord thy God with all thy heart, and thy neighbor as thyself." According to the Apostle, the essence of sin was not in the outward act, but the inward selfishness. It was in the absence of love.

This is the kind of sin which we are very apt to forget or ignore. This love is the one thing needful. "He who loves is born of God," and "he who is born of God doth not commit sin." But "he who loveth not, knoweth not God," and "abideth in death" and fear and weakness. If therefore we do not feel this want of love, we feel really that we have *no sin*, for we ignore the very fact which makes the essence of sin.

§ 52. *How Men say they have no Sin.*

We may now see how it is that this inward ignorance of sin may *express itself* in outward conduct. There are various ways in which men express themselves. We may say things in words, in looks, in actions, in omissions. We may even say one thing in word and another thing in action; and in this case, according to the proverb, the action speaks louder than the word. We may thus contradict ourselves without knowing it, or, as the Apostle says, "deceive ourselves." We deceive *ourselves*, not others. We do not deceive man, we cannot deceive God. What we say with our lips, is what we think we believe, — we believe it with our superficial opinion, — we believe it in the upper strata of our mind. But, meantime, it may easily be that we think the opposite in our deepest conviction, — a conviction so deep that we are not aware of it ourselves. But this deeper conviction will also express itself, not in our words to be sure, but in our conduct, tone, manner. Thus it will often happen that a man will say one thing, and think it too, with his superficial thought, while he is saying the exact opposite with the deeper stress of his inmost nature, will, heart, and conduct.

Thus, to give a familiar instance, many a man says he is a democrat. He professes to be one, and thinks he is one. He belongs to the democratic party; votes the democratic ticket; makes democratic speeches; perhaps declaims loudly in favor of human rights and universal liberty, and against aristocracy and monopoly. But, meantime, *in his heart* he is just the opposite; he is a thorough aristocrat; he really wants only freedom for himself, monopoly for himself, wealth, station, office, power, for himself. Give him these, and he directly shows himself to be an aristocrat of the first water, having no sympathy at all with the poor and oppressed. Yet he did not know that this was his character; he thought himself a democrat. But while his opinions and words said that, his conduct said that his deepest conviction was quite other.

There are then two ways of saying a thing. We say with our lips what we think we believe; we say with our conduct what we really believe. Who, then, are they who say with their conduct that they have no sin?

The Pharisee says, I have no sin. The Pharisee is the man who substitutes the body of religion for its soul, who substitutes outward goodness for inward goodness. The Jewish Pharisee substituted ceremonies and ritual service for justice and mercy. He stood by himself and prayed, and said, God, I thank thee that I am not as other men are. He had made clean the outside of the cup and the platter, and he did not remember that it might be full of evil within. He believed himself to be a very good man, and was so believed to be by others. But Jesus said that he was a hypocrite, and showed him the inward blackness of his heart. Now there are Christian Pharisees as well as Jewish Pharisees, and their character is the same; the distinctive trait being that they make goodness an outside thing altogether. For Christianity has a soul and a body. Its soul is Truth and Love, its body is the outward manifestation of Truth and Love in the form of churches, ceremonies, worship, creeds, sacred books, sacred days, sacred places, sacred speech and action. When we lay an exclusive stress upon the soul of religion, and forget and neglect the body of religion, we become mystics. When we lay an exclusive stress on the body of religion, and forget the soul, we become Pharisees. We also see that there may be various kinds of Pharisees. There is the ceremonial Pharisee, to whom the outward church and visible worship is the whole of religion; there is the orthodox Pharisee, to whom the true creed is the essential thing in Christianity; and there is the moral Pharisee, to whom the outside of decent moral conduct makes the whole of religion. But all these Pharisees agree in thinking themselves free from sin. As a matter of form, they may call themselves sinners, but they do not really believe themselves so. The ceremonial Pharisee regards as sinners the non-professors, — the world's people, — those who laugh and dance and make merry, — those who do not belong to the true Church, — heretics and dissenters. He knows no sin but ceremonial sin, and that he does not commit. So he says, have no sin. In like manner the orthodox Pharisee, who makes Christianity consist in believing the right creed, considers himself free from sin so long as he holds the true doctrine. If a dying man mutters something about atonement and the blood of Christ, he immediately concludes that everything is right. He may himself have nothing of the spirit of Jesus; he may be hard, unforgiving, and full of inward evil, yet he does not notice this, but is only anxious to keep hold of the sound letter of doctrine. But there is another kind of Pharisee, to whom Christianity consists in decent outward conduct, in good behavior, no matter what is its motive. Now, as their deportment may be very fair, and as the world does not condemn them, they really regard themselves as free from sin, only a little imperfect, not as good as they might be. They have never seen their inward bondage to the law of self. And when they speak of sinners, they mean drunkards, and robbers, and characters of that class. All of these three kinds of Pharisees say, by their spirit and conduct, that they have no sin.

Again, the unforgiving man says, I have no sin. I once heard of a New Zealand chief, who, when he recited the Lord's prayer, always said,

"Forgive us our trespasses, though we do not forgive those who trespass against us." That was at least honest and frank. But when we, who know what the Christian rule is, are harsh, relentless, and unforgiving, we show that we do not really believe ourselves to be sinners. For the consciousness of our own inward emptiness and evil would make it impossible to look with severity upon the faults of others.

Again, he who excuses or justifies himself says virtually, I have no sin. The habit of making excuses is opposed both to humility and to truthfulness. It is a region half-way between the land of truth and the land of falsehood. A very truthful person never makes excuses, for this turns away the attention from the main point at issue, and confuses, more or less, moral distinctions. But he who has acquired the habit of making excuses, systematically looks away from his own wrong act in his search for extenuating circumstances. These circumstances can always be found. For no one ever acts without temptation, and the temptation is made the excuse. So that at last the person who makes excuses never feels himself to blame for anything, because there was always some temptation to which he yielded. Thus all sense of sin disappears out of the mind, and instead of feeling guilty, one comes to feel as if he were the injured party, as if he ought rather to be pitied than to be blamed, and as if he had a right to complain of Providence, and be angry with the Almighty, for exposing him to such temptations. Thus a habit of making excuses is the same thing as saying, I have no sin, and is inconsistent with strict truthfulness, concientiousness, and humility.

Again, a man who does not watch — the careless man — says, I have no sin. For a sense of danger makes us watchful. Few men sleep quite as soundly in a steamboat on the Mississippi, as they do in their own bed at home. When an enemy is near, we place sentinels and establish outposts and keep on the alert. If we have a powder-magazine, we are careful to protect it against fire and lightning. Those who live near Vesuvius watch the sounds and the vapor and smoke which come from it, lest, on a sudden, its serene quiet may be changed into destructive activity. But we who have within a sleeping volcano of passions, tendencies to selfishness and worldliness, and the love of money, of power, of pleasure, which may burst forth and sweep us away as others have been swept away, — how is it possible for us to be careless? If we do not watch, it is because we do not realize this danger, nor believe that we have such tendencies. In other words, it is because we say, We have no sin.

Again, the man who *does not pray* says, by that conduct, I have no sin. Whenever we are conscious of danger and evil, we instinctively cry for help. In the moment of shipwreck, even the atheist cries out to God, and the blasphemer turns from cursing to prayer. I never yet saw a person on a death-bed who was not glad to have me pray with him. In that solemn hour, moving on every moment, with irresistible stress, toward the great change, those who were in life the most worldly wish to pray. They forget all their old theories about the uselessness of prayer. A profounder instinct sweeps away these objections. And, in like manner, many persons in life never pray in earnest until they become conscious of sinfulness. The awakened sinner cries out to God. It is impossible to bear the burden of conscience without praying. And therefore, if one does not pray, it is evident that he does not believe himself seriously and really a sinner. This is the way men say they have no sin.

§ 53. *Confession of Sin, and its Results.*

We now ask, in the *first* place, *What is Confession?* And, in the *second* place, we must ask, *How does it procure pardon and salvation?*

Confession, certainly, does not mean merely *saying* that we are sinners. A person may no doubt repeat the Litany, and call himself a miserable sinner ever so often, without really confessing his sin. He must not only *call* himself a sinner, but also *see* that he is a sinner. That is, he must be his own judge, critic, and censor, — keep an eye upon himself, — have a true standard of action before his eyes, and walk according to it. All this is implied in the sight of our sins. But there is something more implied in confession even than this. It is not enough that we see our sins and admit them. True confession also implies that we *feel* them. A merely intellectual recognition may be cold. It is necessary to realize the *sinfulness* of sin, to see that it is *really* SIN, not merely folly or fault or imperfection; to see it as something odious and detestable. For, otherwise, we do not see it as *sin* at all, — not as an offence against God, but only as something injurious to ourselves or to our neighbor.

We may therefore define confession as consisting of three parts. First, the *sight* of our sins. Second, the *feeling* of their sinfulness; and, in the third place, some kind of *utterance*, *manifestation*, or *expression* of this conviction and feeling.

And yet, now that we have thus made out our definition, it would seem to be inadequate. For it does not satisfy the very first illustration which occurs to us. Consider the case of Peter and that of Judas. Peter denied his Master; Judas betrayed him. But Judas, when he found that his Master was condemned, repented himself, we read, "and brought the thirty pieces of silver to the chief priests and elders, saying, 'I have sinned, in that I have betrayed the innocent blood.' And he cast down the pieces of silver in the temple, and departed, and went and hanged himself." Now here, *in the case of Judas*, would seem to be fulfilled our three conditions of true confession. He saw correctly the nature of his sin,—"*I have sinned, in that I have betrayed the innocent blood.*" He openly *expressed* this conviction, both in word and action. And he showed the *depth* of his conviction by taking his own life. This, therefore, would seem to have been a true and perfect confession. And if so, according to the Apostle, God was bound by his own faithfulness and justice to forgive Judas, and to cleanse him from all unrighteousness. But his despair shows that he was not forgiven. And if he had been cleansed from all unrighteousness, instead of taking his life, he would have devoted it to preaching the Gospel.

On the other hand, there is the case of Peter. He does not seem to have made a true confession at all, and yet HE *was* forgiven. He saw and felt his sin indeed. But he made no open or public avowal of it. He went out and wept bitterly. But he did not retract his denial, or declare manfully that he was a follower of Jesus. His subsequent life, indeed, was an open avowal of the truth; but the purpose and intention seems to have been, in his case, already accepted for the act. For we find him already, at the time of the resurrection, in the company of the other disciples again, and restored to his old place in the Master's household.

There is something, therefore, in true confession, besides what we have intimated. And this is the spirit, which makes it a Christian confession or the contrary. The spirit may be either that of despair, like that of Judas, or of trusting hope, like that of Peter. And this spirit, more than the outward manifestation, constitutes the essence of true confession.

The question therefore arises, What is the spirit of confession? And this is best known by means of illustrations.

In the seventh chapter of Luke, there is the story of the woman who brought a box of ointment and anointed therewith the feet of Jesus, washing them with her tears, and wiping them with the hair of her head. She did not say a word, but her actions expressed the tenderness of her heart. The spirit of confession was, in this case, the spirit of LOVE. And so her sins were forgiven.

Again, in the story of the Pharisee and Publican, the Publican, who stood afar off, and did not lift up his eyes to heaven, and smote upon his breast, saying, "God be merciful to me a sinner," was justified or forgiven. In this case, his confession took an outward form, and expressed itself in an open humility. The spirit of confession was here a spirit of HUMILITY.

So, in the parable of the Prodigal Son, there was an open confession, accompanied with the signs of humility and the evidences of sincere penitence. The spirit of confession, in this case, was a spirit of *humility*, *repentance*, and REFORMATION.

Again, in the story of the two sons, one of whom when told to go and work, said that he would go, but did not, and the other refused to go, but afterwards repented and went, it is apparent that the action of the last was equivalent to a confession that he had done wrong. In this case, the spirit of confession was a spirit of AMENDMENT.

The spirit of confession, therefore, implies the presence of humility, love, and a purpose of improvement. The outward form which it assumes may be a form of words, of silent tears, or of conduct without either words or tears. But a noble-hearted person wishes always, when convinced of error or evil, to manifest in some outward way, either by word or action, this consciousness. It is not enough that he feels convinced, he wishes to express that conviction, or, as we say, to unburden himself. He must do something to show his change of conviction and feeling. The simplest mode of confession is, no doubt, in words. Yet one may sometimes feel that actions will speak louder than words; words are more liable to be misunderstood than actions. But a sincere penitence will certainly manifest itself in some way. It wishes to come to the light. It feels that it is due to truth that it should bear its testimony in her behalf. If its past conduct has tended to discredit justice and righteousness, it wishes now to make an open atonement, and to avow different convictions and ideas. A man may secretly change his conduct from wrong to right; having wronged another, he may privately make restitution; but this will hardly satisfy his own conscience. It is not yet a complete repentance.

We sometimes see instances of sums of money being returned through the post-office, or by the hands of a priest, to a person who has been defrauded. In these cases, I think we feel that the repentance is not entire; that there is something else still to be done. And this is an objection against the whole Roman Catholic system of confession, — that it substitutes a half-confession for a whole one. It is a compromise with conscience. The man who has injured his neighbor, and has done harm to society in various ways, and who has not the courage openly to admit his faults to the injured party and to others, compromises by telling the priest, whom he knows to be bound to secrecy. I do not think that the absolution of the priest will enable him to feel that he is forgiven by God. There is still something wanting to the completeness of the atonement.

And now we are prepared to ask, why it is that true confession procures pardon and freedom from sin; why it is that, if we confess our sin, God is faithful and just to forgive us our sin.

There is something peculiar in the statement of the Apostle John. It is singular that it should be said, that forgiveness comes from the faithfulness and justice of God, rather than from the Divine mercy. We should have said, "If we repent of our sin, God is merciful and will forgive it." And, in fact, nothing is more frequent, than for theologians to argue, notwithstanding this text, that the sinner, even when repenting, can expect nothing from the Divine justice but punishment. But the Apostle's statement is very distinctly to the contrary. What are we to understand by it?

We are certainly *not* to understand that confession has any magical quality, nor that this is an *arbitrary* enactment of the Divine will. God's justice and faithfulness mean his fidelity to the laws of his own nature. It is the very law of the Divine nature which is pledged to the forgiveness of him who confesses his sin. By confession, he puts himself in accordance with the nature of things; and the permanency of the Divine nature and government is his pledge that he shall be pardoned and saved.

Jesus has declared that there is nothing covered which shall not be revealed, neither anything hid which shall not be known. This is a law of the Divine government. Everything must come to the light, either willingly or unwillingly, whether it be good or whether it be evil. When evil comes willingly to the light and judges itself, it is confession. When it comes unwillingly, it is judgment. Evil must therefore either confess itself, or it must be judged. We feel the righteousness of this, — that evil ought not to hide itself for ever from the light. Our sense of justice requires that it should be exposed; that it should not wear the garb of virtue; that it should not seem triumphant and plausible always. In the case of others, we see this very plainly. When a bad man — a hard, selfish man — succeeds in his enterprises, tramples upon the rights of others with impunity, and acquires so much power that no one dares to rebuke him, but, instead, he is surrounded with flatterers who justify his course, what do we wish? what do we demand of the Infinite Justice? Not, I think, *punishment*, so much as JUDGMENT. We wish that he should be made to see himself as he really is, and that he should be seen by others as he really is, that he should be exposed in his true character; and that being done, we ask nothing further. We do not ask or wish for any punishment beyond this. But this we ask, not in any personal or private interest, but in the interests of truth and justice. And if, instead of this, he should come to recognize his own evil, and should voluntarily confess and deplore his wickedness, and make what atonement was in his power, the sense of justice will be equally satisfied, and we should demand nothing more.

Now the doctrine of the New Testament teaches that precisely this is the law of the Divine nature and the Divine government. We must either confess or be judged. We must either see our sins ourselves, and show, by a change of conduct and manner, that we see them, which is confession, or else we may be sure that the working of an inevitable law will manifest them openly, either in this life or in the other, to ourselves and to all. And this is judgment. This is the judgment of which Paul speaks when he speaks of the day in which God shall judge the secrets of men by Christ Jesus. The doctrine of judgment to come is a great and permanent doctrine of the New Testament, and is founded on the very nature of things. God is in his nature Light, essential Light. To come to God is to come to the

Light, and to come to the Light is to come to God. As the seed tends to the light, as the bud unfolds toward the light, so the process of human development consists in unfolding and developing from within the soul all that is there, both good and evil. Every step in human life is a step in this process of development. The external world with its beauty and variety tempts forth our faculties and powers. All education is the bringing out or educing that which is within. Labor and study, pleasure and pain, success and failure, sorrow and bereavement, temptation and sin, all reveal man to himself. If he passes through all these experiences in the love of truth, not deceiving himself, but judging himself as he would judge others, he constantly advances nearer to God and to eternal life. But if he says he has no sin, if he excuses and justifies himself, hardens himself against the truth, and makes his will his law, then he makes it necessary that he should be judged by that divine law of God. A judgment of shame, remorse, and anguish is the best thing for him who refuses to judge himself by a healthy and purifying confession of his evil.

If we confess our sins, God is faithful and just to forgive us our sins. What is this forgiveness which comes as the necessary and inevitable consequence of confession? It is the inward sense of reconciliation, the taking away of all estrangement, the Father's love shed abroad in the heart, the removal of every inward barrier or wall of division. This wall of division is solely our own wilfulness of choice, — our determination to see things as we choose, and not as they are, which is equivalent to loving darkness rather than light. But when we love darkness, we thereby turn away from God, and immediately feel ourselves alienated from his love and life. Our heart is cold and hard. We are in a far country, under a sense of the Divine displeasure. But when we look again at the truth, and by the sight and confession of sin return to God, the barrier falls. Love flows in, attended by peace and hope. The day grows beautiful and serene, the air is filled with the love of God. All is cheerful, bright, and fair. Thus it is, that, if we confess our sins, the laws of the Divine nature, which are God's faithfulness and justice, make it inevitable that our sins shall be forgiven.

But there is one step more. The promise is not only that we shall be forgiven our sin, but also that we shall be cleansed from all unrighteousness. A true confession saves us not only from the guilt, but also from the power, of evil,

This is the great hope set before us in the Gospel, of an entire redemption from sin. Nor is there anything unnatural or arbitrary in this. The self-will and pride which refuse to see and admit their evil, prevent the possibility of improvement. But the humility which opens the heart to God's love, which gives the peace of reconciliation, which creates a thankful gratitude, is an infinite power in the soul, of progress and purity. This love makes all things new, casts out all demons of selfishness and worldly desire, and by sweet gradations cleanses the soul from all unrighteousness, until we can say that God's will is ours, and adopt the language of the hymn:—

"I worship thee, sweet Will of God,
 And all thy ways adore,
And every day I live, I long
 To love thee more and more.

"All that God blesses is our good,
 And unblest good is ill;
And all is right that seems most wrong,
 If it be His dear will.

I have no cares, O blessed Will,
 For all my cares are thine;
I live in triumph, Lord! for thou
 Hast made thy triumphs mine."

§ 54. *The Soul's Assurance.*

Few more important questions can be asked, among those which have two sides, than "Can we know that we are Christians? Can we have an assurance that our sins are forgiven us, that we are of the Truth, that we are truly converted, really regenerated? Can we know that we have such a measure of faith, such a degree of religious experience, such sincerity, such piety, such holiness, that we may call ourselves the children of God?"

This question, I have intimated, has two sides; many would, perhaps, answer it in the negative; I answer it unhesitatingly in the affirmative. I believe, not merely that we *can* have this assurance of heart towards God, but that we *ought* to have it, and that there is some serious defect in our religious experience, or some sad error in our mode of thinking, if we are destitute of this confidence. If we do not *know* that we are Christians, it is either because we really are not Christians, or because we have been taught that we *cannot* know it, and so have left off trying to know it. I wish therefore to show that every true Christian *can know* that he is a true Christian, and *ought* to know it.

I do not mean that we ought to think ourselves very good ; the better a man is, the more he sees of his defects and sins. I do not mean that we should believe ourselves very religious, holy, or pure ; if we *are* so, we shall see how little it all is compared with what we ought to be. Nor do I mean that we can or ought to feel sure of salvation, — sure of going to heaven. As long as we live, we are in danger of falling ; as long as we live, we must work out our salvation with fear and trembling, and give diligence to make our calling and election sure. Nor do I mean to say that we can be sure of being right in our religious opinions ; I wish to open no door for dogmatism. People often say, "I am sure I am right, and that 's all I want to know about it." But this assurance of which I speak, does not relate to opinion or belief, — it is an assurance of the heart before God, not of the head. Of this other kind of assurance, which leads people to think their creed certainly right, they have quite enough already.

But what I mean is briefly this, — that we can be sure that we are *on the right way ;* not sure that we have attained salvation, but sure that we can attain it ; not sure that we have attained all truth, but sure that we see the essential, central, fundamental truth ; not sure that we love God with all our heart, but sure that we do love him sincerely and really; not sure that we are obedient in all things, but sure that it is our aim and purpose to obey; not sure that our faith and penitence are what they should be, but that we have the germs of true penitence, and the seeds of a right faith. We may know that we have passed from death unto life, — know that, whereas we were once blind, now we see, — know that we are sincere in our purpose and our effort, and that we have a peace and a joy within, from communing with God, which cannot be taken from us.

I do not mean that we can have this assurance, except we seek for it by self-examination and prayer and solitary determination. It is not a *blind* confidence, but an intelligent and thoughtful faith, —a faith in ourselves, which has its root in a faith in God. Such a faith as this is both possible and very desirable.

It is possible for us all to have it. Yet some will say, No, it is not possible. "A person may be deceived," they say; "he may think he is actuated by high motives, when in reality he is influenced by low ones; he may think he loves God, when in fact he is a formalist. Do we not see instances of this every day? If one may be self-deceived, so may another; so may all of us.

We may all think that we are really Christians, when we are not."

In reply to this I say, Undoubtedly, persons *are* deceived in this manner about themselves, continually, and undoubtedly we may be also. But that is not the question; the question is, *Need* we be deceived? Must we be deceived? Is it not our own fault if we are? Is it not because we do not endeavor to be undeceived, — because we are not strict with ourselves, but take it for granted, as a matter of course, that our hearts are right, when we have no evidence of it at all?

Most of us deceive ourselves about our abilities, or our knowledge, or our attainments; but we need not deceive ourselves. It is in our own power, if we choose to understand ourselves aright in these particulars. Just so, I admit that we are very much in the habit of deceiving ourselves about our spiritual condition. But what I contend for is, that we *need not* do so. It is possible for all of us to say with the Apostle, "Hereby *know we* that we are of the Truth, and assure our hearts before Him."

But it may be said, "Does not the Bible declare that the heart is deceitful above all things, and desperately wicked, — who can know it?" I reply, the heart is deceitful, — I admit it; but to the question, "Who can know it?" I answer, God can know it. His eye can see into the deepest recesses of our soul, can trace every winding of our heart; and what *he* sees, that *he* can reveal. And that is the way, and the only way, by which we can truly know ourselves, by communion with God. It is "his spirit that beareth witness with our spirit, that we are the children of God." There is a voice of God which speaks in our soul, to condemn or to acquit us, and whenever we choose to come out from the bustle of our noisy life, and look into ourselves, we can see what is the language of that voice. What did Paul mean when he said, "Herein do I exercise myself, to have always a conscience void of offence toward God and toward men"? Was it not possible for him to *know* whether his conscience was void of offence? What did he mean by saying, "My conscience bearing me witness in the Holy Ghost," — by "having peace with God through our Lord Jesus," — by "having the love of God shed abroad in our hearts by the Holy Ghost," — or by exhorting believers to "draw near to God with a true heart, in full assurance of faith"? In fine, except it be possible to know that we are Christians, who has a right to any of the promises addressed to Christians in the New Testament?

If, then, it be possible to have this assurance, certainly it is also very desirable to have it. On this point let us dwell, for I think that many do not sufficiently perceive the vast spiritual advantage which comes to us from a cheerful, confident faith, and a well-founded, intelligent hope; nor do they understand the spiritual weakness which is the sure result of perpetual anxiety and doubt concerning our own inward condition. It seems to me to be the one essential blessing of Christianity, that it can inspire this confident trust in the love of God; that it can clear away all doubts, ease the pangs of sin, extinguish the agonizing fires of remorse, and open a path from earth to heaven before the feet of the just, — a path shining more and more unto the perfect day.

We are saved by faith. This is the great assertion, for ever true. It is faith which saves the soul, — faith in God, in truth, in goodness, in the power of love, — yes, faith in ourselves. It is faith which saves us; not the faith of the theologian, reasoning out his sublimely subtile and incomprehensible dogmas, not the cold belief of the bigot in his dusty creed; but the faith of the martyr, upborne amid the flames by confidence in a great principle, — the faith of Stephen, to whom, as the earth was closed, the heavens were opened.

"He heeded not reviling tones,
Nor sold his heart to idle moans,
Though cursed, and scorned, and bruised with stones:

But looking upward, full of grace
He prayed, and from a happy place
God's glory smote him on the face."

Nothing but such a faith as this, — a sight of spiritual things, a clear inward knowledge of God's love, an assurance of pardon, and of an ever-present divine help, — nothing but this could have given the early Christians strength to struggle against the stormy ocean of opposition and hatred which raged around them. No mere belief in Christ founded on argument or evidence; no strong probability that he was from God; no weight of logical demonstration; no speculative persuasion of the truth of Christianity; no hope of a future heaven, a distant immortality, and a final rescue from sin, — could have enabled them to withstand the fearful pressure which bore upon them from all quarters. The rancorous hatred of the Pharisees, and the iron arm of Rome, were no mere probabilities; the dungeon, the cross, the scourge, were no matters of speculation, belief, or logic; slander, abuse, the alienation of friends, the triumph of foes, — these were not distant expectations, they were all stern daily realities. To resist them was needed, not a vague belief, but an assurance, a knowledge, a personal experience of spiritual joy. This was given, and in the strength of this faith, in the consciousness of a heavenly inheritance, a divine friendship, and a present salvation, all external trial became as the light dust of the balance. This faith in a love of God, which they had seen and felt, not which they hoped for, — this it was which was the strength of the early Church.

We need no less now. We need to *know* that God loves us; we need to be *sure* that we are in the right way; we need to *feel* that our sins are forgiven, and that we are the children of God. With such a conviction clear and strong in our hearts, duty is pleasure, trial is happiness. Without it, how hard to struggle against sin, how hard to make daily resolutions, strive with daily temptations, begin continually an ever-recurring warfare! It is too discouraging; sooner or later we must give up in despair.

Still it may be objected, "Is there not danger of encouraging false hopes, self-righteousness, and presumption, by this doctrine? Are not humility and self-distrust recommended in the New Testament? Was not the Pharisee who thought himself good reproved, and the publican who saw his sinfulness commended? Does not Paul recommend, that we should not think of ourselves more highly than we ought to think?"

Certainly, we should not think of ourselves more highly than we ought, but perhaps neither should we think *less* highly. The New Testament teaches Christians to take at once very lowly and very lofty views of themselves, — lowly views of their attainments, lofty of their position and prospects; to be humble when they look at what *they* have done, hopeful when they look at what God has done. The self-righteous man has a foolish confidence in himself the Christian a wise confidence in God; the hope of one rests on an inward fancy, that of the other on an inward fact.

On the other hand, the doctrine we have been advocating, while it is full of comfort to those who are ready to examine themselves, and to seek for the witness of the spirit, is full of warning to those who are careless and indifferent. It says to them: If you do not know that you are Christians, there is reason to believe that you are not so. If you have no inward knowledge of the love of God, you are probably not yet a true disciple of Jesus. There is still a work for you to do: you are still to be born of the spirit, — you still need the baptism of the Holy Ghost.

But how can we attain this assurance? The first thing is, to believe that it can be attained; then we shall make it our object to attain it. Believe then that you can know you are sincere, that you can know you are of the Truth, that you can know your sins are forgiven, that you can know that your prayers are heard and answered. To know that you are sincere, examine yourself, look inward; see if you have any hunger and thirst after righteousness, see if you desire to become holy. If you find that you have this desire, that you are not satisfied with outward comfort and outward success so long as your soul is not right, then you will know that you are in earnest in the pursuit of a divine life. Why should not we say with the Apostle's boldness, "My rejoicing is this, the testimony of my conscience, that in simplicity and godly sincerity, not with fleshly wisdom, but by the grace of God, I have had my conversation in the world"? Let one become assured, by a faithful examination of his own heart before God, that he is sincere, and he will feel strong and happy. Then to know that we are of the Truth, — to be convinced that we have essential truth, that we are not following a cunningly devised fable in following Christ, — to be sure of this, we do not need to study books on the evidences of Christianity; for these, by their own confession, can only give probability. But we should try Christianity itself, live by it, trust in it, look to Christ for a revelation. Then, if we find that he does bring us to God, we shall be sure that he is a mediator; if we find that he does reveal God to us, we shall know that he was sent to reveal God. If we find that he is saving us from our sins, giving us strength and hope, making the trials of this world light, and the hopes of the other world near, then we shall know that he is a Saviour. If, in fine, we are made by him to be at one with God, we shall be sure, without caring to study the controversies about the doctrine of atonement, that we have the essential truth of it. I do not mean that investigation, inquiry, and study of these subjects are unnecessary or unimportant, but I say that they are all secondary to the experimental knowledge of Christ, which comes to us from applying Christianity to our daily life.

Then, once more, we need to know that our sins are forgiven. And how shall we know this? By feeling that we have peace with God, — by feeling that we are able so to trust in the divine compassion and infinite tenderness of our Father, as to arise and go to him, whenever we commit sin, and say at once to him, "Father, I have sinned; forgive me." To know that we are forgiven, it is only necessary to look at our Father's love till it sinks into our heart, to open our soul to him till he shall pour his love into it; to wait on him till we find peace, till our conscience no longer torments us, till the weight of responsibility ceases to be an oppressive burden to us, till we can feel that our sins, great as they are, cannot keep us away from our Heavenly Father, and are able to say, "There is now no condemnation to them that are in Christ Jesus."

And, lastly, we need to know that God hears our prayers. It is not enough to believe that he does, — to think it probable. We need to know, from our own experience, that when we ask anything according to his will, he will give it to us. It is this alone which can establish and make strong the habit of prayer. We ought to be able to say, from our own knowledge and experience, that we shall always gain light, strength, comfort, and joy by drawing near to God in prayer. This will bind us by a golden chain of faith and confidence to the spiritual world, it will be the dearest treasure of our souls, a possession of which no one can ever rob us, a comfort which will pour light on the darkest hours of life.

Of this let us be sure. We do not have half the comfort we might have in our religion, because of a false humility, which not only distrusts itself, which it often ought to do, but also distrusts God, which it never ought to do. Because we have not comfort in our religion, we are also deficient in strength; for I repeat, and wish to repeat, now and for ever, that faith, confidence, hope, and joy in God, are the sinews of all goodness, the strength of all manly virtue, and that doubt, anxiety, fear, and inward uncertainty are the strongest allies of whatever evils war against the soul.

§ 55. *The Soul's Content.*

The Apostle tells us, "I have learned, in whatsoever state I am, therewith to be content." But is contentment always so good a thing? Have we any right to be contented with every state in which we are? Ought we not often to be discontented? That we ought to be discontented with ourselves, with our attainments, our accomplishments, our efforts, our virtues, is very evident. Self-dissatisfaction is the spur to progress. Robert Hall said, "I am constantly tormented with the desire to preach better sermons than I can." Because he was so tormented, he preached better sermons than any man alive. Paul was not contented with himself or his accomplishments. Elsewhere he declares that he does not count himself to have attained, but, forgetting what is behind, he presses forward to that which is before.

Yes, you may say, but what he speaks of here is his outward condition. He had learned to be contented with that; he knew how to be full, and how to suffer want; that is what he is speaking of, — that is the contentment he recommends. True, but this does not quite remove our difficulty. For the question is, Is *contentment* a good and right state of mind, or is it not? Does the old poet say truly,

> "When all is done and said, in the end thus you shall find
> He most of all doth bathe in bliss who hath a quiet mind"?

If contentment is a good state of mind, is it not bad to be discontented even with one's self? And if dissatisfaction with our attainments is a spur to progress and effort, is not dissatisfaction with our condition also a necessary spur to industry and labor? Where would the world, where would civilization be, if all men were just as willing to be poor as to be rich, — to be in beggary and hunger and nakedness, as in competence, — to be destitute of the means of gratifying their tastes, as to possess them? Is not the main difference between the highest civilization of Europe, and the lowest barbarism of Africa, merely this,—that the European is constantly struggling to improve his outward condition, while the African is contented to live in a hovel, to go half-naked, and eat roots and fruit? If civilization, culture, refinement, knowledge, are desirable, then the means for their attainment are also desirable; and among these, none are more essential than dissatisfaction with our outward position, for this is the root and first spring of all civilization.

We very often hear it said that the right way to attain contentment is to reduce our desires within the smallest limits. If we wish for very little, we shall be satisfied with very little. "*Have few wants*," is preached to us continually by the most eminent moralists. An Italian beggar, who only wishes to lie in the sun and eat maccaroni, has fewer wants than an enterprising New-Englander. Asia has fewer wants than Europe,—Africa than Asia. A dog has fewer wants than a man, for the savage needs a hut and some few tools and weapons, while the dog needs only a hole in the ground, and liberty to roam after his prey. A tree has fewer wants than a dog, for it only wants to stand still and have sunshine and air around its head, earth and water around its roots. And a stone has the fewest wants of all, for it needs only a place to lie in. Now a system of morals which tends *downwards* in this way, and the legitimate logical result of which would be to make us wish for the condition of a stone, cannot be founded in truth and reason.

Moreover, if we should reduce our desires to the smallest limits, and come to live a hermit life on a little bread and water, wrapt in a coarse cloth, and dwelling in a little cell, still I doubt if true contentment would be thereby attained. The discontent which quarrels with outward things is symptomatic. Men are discontented with their outward position, because they are dissatisfied with their inward state. They know they need something, and they cannot be contented till that something is attained; but they think that what they want is a little more money, a better house, more praise, more power, this office, that situation. If they have them, they will not be contented, — if they make up their mind to do without them, they will not be contented; for the root of their discontent remains within their own mind. Like the man in a fever, who tosses from side to side of his couch, hoping to find an easier position, when the cause of his restlessness is not in his position, but in himself, so the discontented man will be discontented until he is cured of his disease. Surrounded with every luxury that wealth can purchase or ingenuity invent, he is still discontented, restless, dissatisfied; or if poor and destitute, he is envious, repining, and covetous. Contentment comes neither from poverty nor from riches, it comes from the state of the soul, and flows from within out.

The problem of contentment, then, is this, — to be contented with our present position whatever it may be, and yet endeavor to improve it and make it better; — to be contented in poverty while in it, and yet hope to rise above it, — to be contented while ignorant, and yet seek for knowledge; — to say always, "I have enough," yet be willing to receive more, if God sees fit to open the way for it; — in short, not to lay much stress, one way or the other, on our outward position, but to have the fountain of contentment within, in a full and active soul.

Such contentment is not sluggishness, not the contentment of a stone, not the absence of desire, not the insensible unprogressive condition of a savage. A man may be contented where he is, because he is conscious that he is full of life, and must make progress. A man may be contented to be poor in this world's goods, because he is so rich in powers of thought and affection, capable of ample enjoyment in the activity of his mind and heart.

True contentment is noble. It is the perfect poise of a well-balanced mind; of a healthy nature; of one who has no vague wishes, no inconsistent wants; who knows what he would have and how to attain it; who can wait when patience is necessary and work when work is timely, not daunted by failure, not elated by success. Such content comes as the ripe fruit of long experience. "I have *learned*," says Paul, "in whatsoever state I am, therewith to be content." It is not a gift of nature or grace, not a constitutional endowment, but something to be acquired by struggle. It is not the fruit of conversion, for Paul, though converted, had to learn it. And now let us see how it is learned.

We learn to be contented with our situation, when we see how independent of situation are all the great blessings of life, — that real happiness is not given to any select circle or private class. God's great gifts are Love, Knowledge, Truth, and Goodness, and these are everywhere, — they are not monopolized by any rank or sphere of society.

How many a miserable room in our cities is made dear and precious by the love which inhabits it! How many a splendid house is dwelt in by cold and unsympathizing hearts! Which makes the best home, love or fine parlors? It is the smile of welcome, it is the warm grasp of a friend's hand, it is the cordial sympathy, which alone makes a home out of brick and mortar; and these are to be found among the rich and the poor alike. So it is with sagacity, knowledge, insight; — how little do these depend on circumstances! Sir Robert Peel's father gave his son fifty thousand dollars a year to begin life with Benjamin Franklin had nothing; but both became men of rare sagacity. Universal as the air which enters the palace and the cottage, — as the sunlight which sleeps on the smoky rafters of the one, and illuminates the marbles and mirrors of the other, — love and knowledge, truth and goodness, find their way into the hearts and minds of men and women in all classes, in all situations. In the uneducated we often see a native refinement and purity which come direct from God; often in the educated we find only a polished coarseness, a civil selfishness, — mean thoughts and low aims. And yet we often see among the opulent and fashionable less of aristocracy, and more real humanity and democracy, than among those less favored, — they are simple, unpretending, and humble. So among the uneducated and poor, we find a noble dignity of character, self-respect, and true refinement. These things are independent of situation, they depend on character.

So, too, we learn to be content where we are, by finding how equal are the trials of life;

> "To each their sufferings, — all are men,
> Condemned alike to groan."

Addison, in the Spectator, tells a dream, in which he imagined that it was decreed by Jupiter that all unhappy persons might change their troubles with each other. So all began immediately to trade away their calamities. One man exchanged his poverty for a fit of sickness; one gave up the gout, and took instead an undutiful son. But very soon they found their new troubles worse than the old to which they had become accustomed, and were very glad to change back again. We often see persons who seem the favorites of Fortune, and others who seem the mark for all her arrows. But when we look closer, we see drawbacks and compensations. There is always a fly in the ointment, always a blessing with the trial. "We are the trees whom shaking fastens more." The fiery trial develops strength and beauty in the character, just as the dikes of lava which broke their way through the rocky strata of the earth changed them as they passed into beautiful marbles and precious gems.

But especially do we learn to be content with our situation, by learning to see God in all things. Where we are, God has placed us; what we have, God has given us. A traveller arrived at the gate of a town late at night, and found it closed; for bands of robbers were in the neighborhood. "What my Father does is good," said he, fastened his horse to a tree, lighted his lantern, and lay down to sleep. In the night a storm came, blew out his light, and his affrighted horse broke his rein and ran away. "What my Father does is good," said he, and went to sleep again. In the morning he went to the town, and found that the robbers had come in the night, broken into it, and carried off the inhabitants. Had he been in it, he had been taken too; and the storm, which extinguished his light, prevented them from seeing him. When we are able to say, "What my Father does is good," we shall have learned, in whatever state we are, therewith to be content.

Again. By living for a good object, we learn

to be content. The root of all discontent is self-love, — the root of true content is work done in love for true ends. He who is usefully employed is satisfied wherever he may be. Whether his work is to dig the foundation, or finish the inner gilding of his master's house, the consciousness of usefulness makes him cheerful and happy. While our heart is in getting, we can never get enough, we can never be satisfied. But if our heart is in giving, in doing good to others, — if we live for that, then there comes a healthy and serene cheerfulness, which spreads joy over life, and makes death, when it comes, welcome, though unwished for.

How many there are in our community surrounded by all the comforts which life can offer, — health, fortune, friends, every opportunity, — who are yet miserable, simply because they have no useful occupation, — because they are not interested in any good work, doing nothing for their fellow-men.

> "Some murmur when their sky is clear,
>   And wholly bright to view,
> If one small speck of dark appear,
>   In their great heaven of blue;
> And some with thankful love are filled,
>   If but one streak of light,

> One ray of God's good mercy, gild
> The darkness of their night."

The reason is, that the one is living for himself alone; the other is living for his brother. This is the soul's contentment, the satisfaction flowing out of a deep spiritual life, — a life hid with Christ in God. This Christian contentment is paired with a Christian discontent, and the one and the other lead us to the mercy-seat of God, and fill us more and more with the SPIRIT OF PRAYER.

THE END.

www.ingramcontent.com/pod-product-compliance
Lightning Source LLC
LaVergne TN
LVHW020216110826
845151LV00003B/733

* 9 7 8 1 4 2 5 5 3 3 8 2 3 *